Louie G. & I joined the FBN New York office at or about the same time in the spring of 1960. Although there were long periods of times we weren't in contact, some 60 years later we are still trusted & close friends.

I can't imagine anyone working undercover for a prolonged period of time, especially in drug infested areas like Louie G. did, being able to maintain his own persona & also keep his family safe & secure at the same time. But that's just what special Agent Gonzalez was able to do. No matter the myriad roles he had to assume for his many assignments, in between & 24/7 he had to be ready to fall back into character at any given moment.

We had some great Agents in NY in the day & none better than Louie G. —his humility is evident as you turn the pages of his adventures—what he lacked in physical stature he made up with his guts & smarts. I was very proud to have worked with Louie— the best part was, when covering him while on assignment, seeing him walk out of a "buy" unharmed & as cool & cocky as he was when he went in—well that's Louie G!!!

A.J. Falanga
Retired New York State Supreme Court Judge

WALKING
the
Tightrope

Reflections of a
Federal Narcotic Undercover Agent

ANGEL L. GONZALEZ

Based on a True Story

The names of some of the characters have been changed to protect their privacy and safety.

<u>Behaviorism</u>:

The theory that man's actions are automatic responses to stimuli and not dictated by consciousness.

Foreword

As you will surmise by this stunning personal history, Angel L. Gonzalez—Louie G, as we call him—outlines his personal triumphs and tribulations with the Federal Bureau of Narcotics, (FBN), later to be called the Drug Enforcement Administration (DEA), and covers a myriad of reasons for his extraordinary rise, development, and advancement within a notoriously insular, bureaucratic organization. This is no surprise, given how he grew up and the tenor of the times when he was raised.

Louie G is an adopted child of Puerto Rican descent, who was raised by a devoted, nurturing mother, who was married to a stern, no-nonsense military man. Louie was raised a single child in Sunset Park, Brooklyn, after his parents left Puerto Rico in the mid 1940's for a better life and settled in New York. Louie G is a product of the New York public school system which entailed rigorous, demanding academic instruction that included civics, classical music and theater, something completely lacking in today's city school system. He had a strong Catholic upbringing which only added to his development.

He was equally adept in the classroom as he was dancing and playing sandlot baseball. This helped him assimilate and later enhanced and helped to facilitate his role as an undercover agent with the Federal Bureau of Narcotics (FBN) in the 1960's. The camaraderie that developed among the kids he grew up with, played ball with, caroused with and met in dance halls would later morph into fast friends which became a constant theme throughout his life.

He was a very normal kid, who loved to dance and play baseball. He has always been a diehard New York Yankees fan, which was "voodoo" in Brooklyn with the hometown Dodgers, as one might assume. A more storied history for an avid New Yorker, no doubt, not unlike his own personal story. He still loves to dance and listen to salsa music. He has always entertained varied interests and intellectual stimulation in many ways. He is a veteran of the US Army and served in postwar Korea.

He wanted to make his parents proud and initially contemplated becoming a police officer with the NYCPD. Although he passed the test, he didn't meet the height requirements at the time. This didn't deter him; instead he focused his energies on becoming among the first few Latino, undercover drug agents ever to work for the Federal Bureau of Narcotics. Needless to say, this was a source of pride and he was enthused to come home and tell his parents of his achievement. But his mother told him to put his badge and gun away and to check his ego and bluster at the door, because it was more important for him to just be himself, like the son that they had raised.

Louie G isn't a big man in stature, but he is a giant in the personal attributes he possesses. Most people don't have the internal fortitude and guts that Lou has. He isn't afraid of anything and is willing to try almost anything. I was amazed to learn that he ran in 13 New York City marathons, several biathlons, and one triathlon, beginning at age 50. He is a man of character, integrity, honesty, strength, street-savvy, personal charm, and he obviously possesses chameleon-like skills and guile at gaining the trust of people, even the bad actors and drug dealers he dealt with over the early stage of his career.

We often talk about his days as an agent with FBN and a truism he got from a mentor that he very much subscribes to: BIG CASES—BIG PROBLEMS, SMALL CASES—SMALL

PROBLEMS, and NO CASES—NO PROBLEMS. Needless to say, Louis G worked BIG CASES because that is the person he is. He did so because he loved it, admired the people he worked for and along with, while totally believing in the overall cause. When the inner workings of the Federal Bureau of Narcotics imploded, Louie G moved on to other pursuits. Louie has faced adversity, endured it, but more importantly, he rose above it.

Subsequent to his days with FBN, he went to work with International Paper Company (a Fortune 500 Company), where he managed a venture capital endeavor that provided capital and technical assistance to small businesses lacking expertise in the field and helped them become more competitive. He helped International Paper Company's Human Resources Department recruit engineers, chemists, and others with technical backgrounds, from the University of Puerto Rico, enabling the company to improve its (EEO) Equal Employment Opportunity posture. He also assisted in the development of a local workforce for Native Americans in the State of Maine and secured Marketing Assistance to the Sioux Nation in the Dakotas.

A graduate of Fordham University at Lincoln Center in New York, Louie G also spent several years with the Department of Defense, conducting background investigations on personnel seeking employment with government agencies such as the Drug Enforcement Administration, the Federal Bureau of Investigation, Central Intelligence Agency, and the U.S. Customs and the CIA.

I met Angel L. Gonzalez; Ango; Angel; or Louie G (whatever you wish to call him) late in his career—his third stage, you could say. I was working for the Horsemen's Association at the (NYRA) New York Racing Association Racetracks (Aqueduct; Belmont and Saratoga Race Course) when my path crossed with Louie's. He was the Investigator for the NYS Gaming

Commission, the agency that regulates all forms of gambling in New York State. The Commission was formerly the NYS Racing and Wagering Board who had been my employer earlier in my career.

We knew one another casually, but I certainly didn't know about the early part of his career with FBN, but I came to know it and totally admire him and his many accomplishments.

I am the son of Irish-born, second-generation immigrants, who was raised by devout Catholic parents who knew the importance of an education, hard work, and who wanted a better life for their kids than they had. My brothers and sister are descendants of the Greatest Generation.

Louie G has traits you don't always find in an Investigator. He has a big heart and always strives to help those less fortunate than himself. He is aggressive, fair, and objective. He'll support the underdog when required or necessary, ensuring that they are not taken advantage of; not an easy requisite for anyone in that position. He's also very tough when dealing with persons of unsavory behavior that are looking to expose weaknesses in the system, evidenced by the cases he made as an agent against major narcotic dealers.

We collaborated to help many on the "Backstretch" at the racetrack(s), primarily Latinos or immigrants from Central and South America, which required assistance with many issues. Louie spoke Spanish, which was a Godsend, and together we worked to dismantle whatever obstacles were in their way. We experienced much success for those people on the backstretch.

Louie G's life has come full circle. He is the devoted father to three grown children, married to a wonderful wife, Eleanor, for over 55 years, and commands the respect of those that know him and continues to make the world a better place for others.

His story and experiences as one of the first Latino agents with the Federal Bureau of Narcotics (FBN) is exciting and intriguing, which doesn't surprise me at all, because Angel L. Gonzalez is one of a kind. He's an extraordinary individual and my very dear friend.

Jim Gallagher,
Formerly Executive Director of the Kentucky Horse Racing Commission

Author's Notes

On Memorization

Forgetfulness is one of the more essential issues we have to deal with as we get older and go through the aging process. The two are not mutually exclusive. No one is exempt, and no one gets a pass. It's a process we all have to go through. However, there's some degree of comfort in knowing that most of us are in the same or similar situation. For instance, we may not remember what we had for dinner yesterday. But, we remember, very clearly and quite vividly, incidents that occurred to us many years ago when we were youngsters that had a remarkable impact in our lives.

Now, I might not remember what I had for dinner yesterday, but I can honestly say that I remember very clearly and vividly an incident that occurred when I was thirteen years old at my parish (St. Michael's Catholic Church) in the Sunset Park section of Brooklyn, where I grew up.

On this particular day, I was at the church with many other youngsters, rehearsing for our Confirmation Ceremony (a religious rite in the Catholic faith). During the actual celebration, there comes a point when the bishop holding Mass will very gently strike each Confirmation recipient on the cheek and then gives you his blessing.

At the rehearsal, Sister Alice Joseph, the nun who was in charge of the event, played the part of the bishop. There was no secrecy or mystery that Sr. Alice Joseph, or The Sheriff as she was called, was the dogmatic leader at the school/church. Sister Alice Joseph's reputation preceded her. It became apparent that there were a number of boys—myself included—whose conduct did not exactly meet nor satisfy the good sister's standard of behavior.

We were in line rehearsing, and as we moved towards the altar, it was my turn to receive the Confirmation Blessing. Sister Alice Joseph, portraying the role of the bishop, proceeded to strike my cheek not once but several times, not gently but rather harshly. The good sister who looked more like a "conductor leading a symphony" was undoubtedly trying to catch up for previously missed opportunities. Needless to say, it was an embarrassing moment for me as I desperately tried to hold back the tears, lest my image be ruined.

Well known as a strict disciplinarian, the sister would probably have defined her behavior as a form of "discipline." There were those, and there are still many, who subscribe to that philosophy. I'm more inclined to believe that the entire episode was not so much an illustration of discipline but a manifestation of the sister's own anger and frustration that was being revealed.

The embarrassing incident was short and quick. And although it occurred a very long time ago, nevertheless, it was a harrowing experience that I have never forgotten nor will I ever forget.

Similarly, the same can be said about the investigations and incidents described in this book, as well as some of the principals involved.

These events took place in the Sixties. It's quite possible, therefore, that an individual's first or last name might have been forgotten or even omitted and a different name may have been used (e.g., Billy instead of Jimmy, or Jones in lieu of Smith). However, the character(s) were real people, the stories are true and that has not changed. The same can be said as to days of the week and the time of day. Incidents may have occurred on a Tuesday instead of a Wednesday and the time might have been 8:00 pm instead of 9:00 pm.

In any event, while a few minor changes may have indeed taken place, there is no doubt as to the authenticity of the events and the individuals involved. Every effort was made to lend credence to the events and maintain the integrity of the investigations by providing a reference page at the end of the book that contains court documents and newspaper articles relative to the investigations.

The cases/investigations described herein were selected for several reasons. First they depict aspects of a narcotic agent's function. They reflect common elements of suspense, intrigue and drama one might expect when living on the edge or working undercover. For instance, the undercover work as illustrated in the Salzano investigation; the foot surveillance and pursuit driving required in the French Connection case and the rigorous cross-examination an agent is often subjected to, as in the Ambassador case. The investigations also included the dark side of undercover work, death threats in particular and an actual murder as in the Salzano Investigation. Additionally, while most cases at the time were made by utilizing informants, others like the Albert Pereida case, were made without the benefit of an informant, but by agent infiltration.

However, the real or most important reason these cases were chosen, was because of the impact they've had in my career and the difference they've made. And that will never be forgotten.

On Names and Nicknames

Since childhood through adulthood, I've used or been called by so many different names, a brief explanation might be necessary.

It all started with my mom (God rest her soul), a wonderful, affectionate woman with strong Catholic beliefs. Consistent with those beliefs, she had great aspirations for her son and named him "Angel." However, her perception of virtue was not validated and her dream did not become a reality. And—truth be told—just the thought of it is frightening.

Growing up in Brooklyn, I played baseball with the neighborhood team, representing the Police Athletic League (PAL) and the local precinct in the area. In our very first game, while writing up the line-up card, one of the coaches asked the manager who was going to play second base. The manager replied, "Angel, the Puerto Rican kid over there," pointing to me.

"What's his name?" The coach asked.

And one of my teammates yelled, "Angel!"

"What was that?" The coach asked.

"Angel," came the response again.

"Not anymore!" Shouted the coach. "From here on in, it's Ango."

"Ango? Why Ango?" I asked.

"Because," the coach said, "first of all, there are no Angels on this team and you're not going to be the exception. Besides, Ango sounds more like a street name, rather than something out of heaven, so that's it, Ango. Now go get a bat. It's batting practice, and I wanna see you hit."

Years later when I became an Agent, I used the name on several undercover assignments. I also had an opportunity to discuss the nickname with Joe Casale, my erstwhile partner. When I explained to him the story of how I came by the name, his immediate response was, "It's a genuine street name without a doubt. And it's also a good name to use undercover. But, friends that we are, I must tell you candidly, "Ango" really sounds like a fuckin'gorilla's name. But I like it. In fact, from now on I'm going to call you "Ango." Inasmuch as you love to dance, we might even choose to call you "Mambo Ango." It has a nice ring to it. Now, you're not going to have a problem with my calling you Ango, every now and then are you?"

"Of course not" I said, you can call me whatever you're comfortable with".

At the time, it was also fashionable for agents to be called by their first names with an emphasis on the first letter of their last name (e.g., Frankie I, Charlie C, Peter P, etc.).

The notion of addressing agents in such fashion made a

number of people curiously wonder if these guys had any last names at all. I had been christened Louie G by Ben Fitzgerald, my very first supervisor and friend. In addition to "Ango," I went on to use other names like Bobby Cubano, Bobby Bright Eyes, and Cano—names given to me by informants/defendants, prior to going out on a case.

In the Latino culture, the nickname "Cano" is quite common. Pronounced (Kano) as Ka in Katherine, it's the equivalent of American nicknames such as "Slim" for the skinny kid, "Red" for the red head and "Freckles" for the freckle faced. In one particular case while working undercover at a Harlem night spot, the informant, who was Latino, introduced me to the defendant in Spanish, saying to him, "This is Cano, the cat [guy] I was telling you about." Later on, when I got the opportunity, I asked the informant why he introduced me as "Cano," and he said, "Well, when we met the other day, I found out your last name is Gonzalez. Well, this guy I'm bringing you to, his last name is Gonzalez and my last name is Gonzalez. That can be confusing, man, and I didn't want to fuck things up, especially if we go to court. Since I didn't know your first name and I forgot to ask you what name you'd be using or what name you wanted me to call you by, Cano was real easy for me. So that's your name from now on, bro."

As it turned out, the informant was right on target, as the case went to court and the issue of names came up, in a comical sort of way, not about "Cano" but Gonzalez. Interestingly enough, the case went to trial. At the commencement of the trial, the judge informed the jurors of what the trial was all about and proceeded to tell them the following: "Ladies and Gentlemen of the Jury. We have a rather unusual situation in court today that I must bring to your attention. Earlier, you heard me say that it was the *United States vs. Robert Gonzalez,* the defendant. It should be noted that the name of the Federal Narcotic agent in this case is Angel

Gonzalez, and the informant who is not here today, his name is David Gonzalez. Therefore, to clear the air and avoid confusion, I will ask Agent Gonzalez to stand up and introduce himself, so you will know who these three individuals are. Agent Gonzalez, would you kindly stand up and introduce yourself to the jury? Thank you." I stood up, waved and nodded to the jurors, and the trial got underway.

Since Cano was the nickname I had used in the case, it often came up during the course of the trial. However, it was the judge's comments on the Gonzalez triad that got the laughs, not on the nickname Cano.

I worked with the informant a few more times on several investigations, and every time we met a different suspect, he continued to introduce me as "Cano" which I later used in other investigations. Thus, another name was added to my list of aliases. But, as Shakespeare said, "What's in a name?"

Acknowledgements

As a first-time writer, I thought long and hard about who to thank for helping me with the book. I began preparing an "Acknowledgements" section and quickly realized that it would probably take several pages because of the countless number of people to thank. I also felt that even upon completion, there would still be someone left out whose feelings would be hurt. And if I discovered I had left someone out, albeit unintentionally, it would create a conflict of conscience that would bother me terribly.

While I was ambivalent about an "Acknowledgements" section, the decision quite candidly, was one of convenience. Therefore, to all those who helped me (they were innumerable), they all know who they are and how deeply grateful I am. Without them, this book could not have been written. To each and every one of them I say, from the bottom of my heart, thank you so much and I love you all.

1

Retirement Dinner Party

It was a cold, rainy day, and the blustering wind made the evening seem much colder than it really was. Despite the inclement weather, there was a large turnout that included my immediate family, friends, and colleagues from the track, my friends from law enforcement, and a few buddies from Sunset Park in Brooklyn, the neighborhood where I was raised. There were also a number of friends from out of town who had made the trip from Saratoga, Boston, New Jersey and Connecticut.

It was, after all, my retirement dinner party. We were celebrating at Stella's, one of the finest Italian restaurants on Long Island, located in Floral Park, a short distance from Belmont Racetrack, my last place of employment.

While the New York Racing Association runs and operates the racetracks in New York, the NYS Gaming Commission regulates all forms of gambling in the State of New York, including thoroughbred and harness racing.

After fifteen years of service, I was retiring from the NYS Gaming Commission as the Track Investigator at their three thoroughbred racetracks in New York (Aqueduct, Belmont Park, and Saratoga).

Linda Williamson and Jimmy Froehlich, friends and colleagues of mine for many years at the racetracks, had done an incredible job of organizing and coordinating the entire event. Linda's categorical table arrangements and juxtaposition of family members, personal friends, and colleagues from the past was remarkable. The tables had been arranged to occupy family members as well as friends from law enforcement, the racetrack, and other professions.

A few people had been called upon to say a few words. Jim Gallagher, a good friend from the racetrack and the emcee, made a very moving speech with some very kind words. Steve Lewandowski, the state steward at the track, had some words of praise and then focused his remarks on a few bizarre incidents we had witnessed that occurred during the licensing process with celebrities from the worlds of sports and entertainment. John Good, a friend and former FBI agent, commented on some experiences we'd both shared while working together in the past. Two of my buddies (Allie and Carlo) from Sunset Park, the Brooklyn community where I grew up, were also present. They still preferred to call me Ango, my neighborhood nickname. Both had arrived early in the day so they could spend some time at the track. They were later joined by my good friend, Louie Lazzinnaro, a highly successful businessman, a horse owner but more importantly, a 'class act.' Louie is also the owner of "NOVE" one of the finest Italian restaurants in Saratoga. He'd made the long trip from Saratoga to join in the celebration.

As they sat together, Carlo had been asked to say a few words. He complied with the request, went to the dais, grabbed the mike and proceeded to dazzle the audience with a couple of anecdotes from the old neighborhood that included some impromptu remarks and "off the cuff" language. Needless to say he brought the house down.

Joe Casale, my erstwhile partner and close friend, followed Carlo and I didn't know what to expect. An eloquent speaker, Joe was well-known for mixing street jargon with his brand of grandiose phraseology. Surprisingly enough, Joe deviated from his intellectual commentary to a more conventional idiom that was full of praise. However, he wasn't done.

As he left the dais he stopped and spoke closely to me. "Ango," he said quietly as he held my hand, "this was a horrible drive just to get here from Greenwich, Connecticut. I had to deal with nothing but bumper to bumper traffic and pounding rain storms. Let me tell you it was a nightmare. Miserable. To come out on a night like this and drive all the way from Connecticut to Long Island is the height of asininity. No one in their right fucking mind would come out on a night like this. It's moronic. But I mean this from the bottom of my heart; I have a very short list of people I would do this for, and brother, you are on the top of that list. I love you my man, you deserve it." As we embraced, I told him how proud I was to have him for a friend.

Immediately after that another good friend and former DEA associate of mine, Paul Doyle, approached me. Paul was an powerful man, built like a NFL defensive lineman, well educated and, though humble by nature, he was tough as nails and someone you could truly rely on. He eventually became the chairman of the Boston chapter of the AFFNA. He also reminded me that he had driven through the same miserable storm all the way from Boston to attend my dinner. He approached me, and with his usual broad smile, said, "Amigo, I'm so glad to be here. This is one celebration I could not miss. Comprende!"

Just seeing him made me even happier. I replied, "Friend, your pronunciation has improved."

The time had come for me to say a few words. Mario Clausell, an old friend and former DEA agent who was also involved in the ceremony, had beckoned me to come up to the dais to accept the plaque normally awarded to those who retire. Mario's authoritative command of "Louie G, it's time brother, front and center," was consistent with his military background.

The presentation of the award by my supervisor, Terry Byrne, a former lieutenant with the NYC Police Department, now

Director of Investigations for the NYS Gaming Commission and his words of praise on behalf of management at the NYS Gaming Commission, made me feel a bit awkward and somewhat embarrassed.

Upon receiving the award, it was time for me to say a few words. I had promised myself to keep the speech to a minimum while at the same time, try to avoid being boring. Not an easy task, but I think I succeeded.

As I walked past the crowd and circled around the room from table to table, it was a great feeling for me to see those I cared for and loved. I hugged and embraced my wife, Eleanor, my daughters, Lianne and Karen, their respective husbands, Joe and Bob, and my son, Skip.

A dose of introspection quickly made me realize what a lucky guy I was and how fortunate I've been to have such a wonderful, supportive family and so many great friends, all of whom had gathered here to join in the celebration.

Everything had gone so well and seemed so perfect. But, as the celebration came to a close, I was still struggling with the notion that my long journey had also come to an end.

After spending approximately fifty-seven years of my adult life working in different professions (law enforcement; education; private industry; and a regulatory agency), it was all coming to an end.

My experience in these various career fields had been very interesting and worthwhile. Each profession had been different and unique in its own way, each with its ebbs and flows, and they all had provided me with a great deal of knowledge and experience. It all felt quite strange now, perhaps because it seemed to have happened so quick and so sudden.

Throughout the years, I shared a myriad of stories, anecdotes, etc. with many different people regarding my past experiences in each of those careers. In sharing those stories, it was interesting to note that most listeners showed vast interest and a preference for the crime stories, particularly narcotics investigations, more than for any other type of story.

When engaged in conversation about a specific story or an anecdote from any of those professions, the questions or comments were generally the same, "That's a great story, write a book." "When are you going to write a book?" or "You gotta write a book." Moreover, when the conversation centered around a specific career, invariably their reaction was, "Which career did you enjoy the most?" "Which one did you prefer?" and "If you had to do it all over again, which one would you choose?" I don't know that these questions can be answered in absolute terms, but one thing I do know for certain. My career with FBN, albeit short-lived, was filled with danger, excitement and intrigue.

Despite the dangerous aspects of the job, the risks involved and the life-threatening situations, I enjoyed being an Agent, oftentimes working around the clock. I worked relentlessly while simultaneously learning from some of the best agents in the agency and some truly incredible experiences.

The allure of the job and the years I spent as an agent were by far the most interesting, insightful, and productive years a person can have in any one career, or lifetime. Thus, I still have a strong and emotional attachment to my role as an undercover agent with FBN, later to be called DEA.

Over the years, as an unwilling and unknowing raconteur, I've been urged and encouraged by a number of people whose judgment I trust and value, to write a book. But, for whatever reason, I've always procrastinated. Now that I had retired, my feeling was that perhaps the time had come to try my hand at writing. Once the decision was made, one question remained. What will I write about?

Inasmuch as the investigation business has been the tapestry woven in my professional life and in view of the emotional attachment to the role of undercover agent, I thought it would be appropriate to start the process where the journey first began - as a federal narcotics agent with FBN. Thus, I could share with the reader an exciting and adventurous part of my life as an undercover agent, while at the same time; highlight some of the more interesting investigations I was involved with early in my FBN career.

2

Background

It all began a very long time ago in New York City (circa August 1960) when I first joined the Federal Bureau of Narcotics (FBN), a predecessor agency of the Drug Enforcement Administration (DEA).

The period of the Sixties was a time of discontent in the U. S. as the country was going through great social, political, and technological change. While on the one hand we witnessed the first manned space flight to the moon and the emergence of the Civil Rights Movement, we also witnessed Malcolm X preaching black superiority and the Black Panthers advocating violence against the police, as the crime rates soared all across the country.

Simultaneously, the use of drugs had become fashionable and widespread. While the drug of choice was marijuana, heroin and cocaine had become equally desirable, albeit both were more dangerous than marijuana.

As the drug problem in the country became more pervasive, a small federal agency, the Federal Bureau of Narcotics (FBN), then under the aegis of the U.S. Treasury Department, continued to wage war against drug trafficking and drug-related crimes.

Located at the old Federal Building at 90 Church Street by the old Twin Towers in downtown Manhattan, FBN was a small federal agency whose sole mission then, was the same as DEA's mission is today: "To combat drug trafficking and drug-related crimes by enforcing violations of the Federal Narcotics and Controlled Substances Laws."

The agency's success in combating the drug traffic, the impact it had on the community, and the blow it dealt to the narcotics underworld was unprecedented, due in large part to the performances of a small group of unforgettable and extraordinary agents.

FBN was made up of approximately four hundred agents nationwide. In New York City alone there were about seventy-five to eighty-five agents. There were approximately five enforcement groups, comprised of fifteen agents per group and a sixth group (Registrants Group) whose main responsibility was the compliance function, to ensure the registration of all physicians who prescribed controlled substances and the pharmaceutical industry who sold them.

Every enforcement group had an assortment of agents with a wide range of personalities, from the sharp, tough, street-talking guy, to the quiet, unassuming and reserved type, to the strange and bizarre.

In each group for instance, there was always a handful of guys who made a mystery out of going to the bathroom. They perceived themselves as CIA agents because in their world, they actually thought they were CIA operatives.

There were others who were even greater enigmas, given the manner in which they conducted themselves. It was difficult for anyone to ascertain who they really were or find out if they were truly agents, politicians, or some government bureaucrat. You often wondered if they themselves knew who they really were.

As in every organization, each group also had its fair share of drones, plus a bizarre few who seemed to have emerged straight out of Barnum & Bailey's Circus. There was always a curiosity or a puzzling perception as to their presence - leading you to wonder - who were these guys, where the hell did they come from, and why were they there to begin with?

It doesn't take a genius to figure out that when you add up the total sum of those parts, you're left with a rather small group of agents that you would like to believe were the real deal.

But make no mistake, that remaining core group was a cadre of dedicated, conscientious, and determined agents who were responsible for approximately forty to fifty percent of the cases prosecuted in the federal courts of New York City, thus making FBN one of the most successful federal agencies in the country at the time.

As a contemporary who worked with these guys during that period, I dare say they were not only amongst the best then, but would still be recognized as the apex in law enforcement and the scourge of the underworld.

There's absolutely no question, nor is there any doubt in my mind, that FBN, and its core group of unforgettable characters, were responsible for "blazing the trail" and putting the DEA on the map.

3

FBN-DEA
(Then and Now)

In order to better understand the nature of the events that took place and the investigations described herein, one should be aware of the essence of the times in which these incidents and investigations occurred. The reader should also have a basic idea as to the differences between FBN then, and DEA now. It was, after all, a different time and a whole different generation. Although a few similarities remain, there are some stark differences. For purposes of clarification, a brief summary might be appropriate.

While the mission of the agency has remained the same, certain changes have taken place over the years that have enhanced DEA's posture, growth, and overall development within the law enforcement community. Organizationally, DEA is currently under the aegis of the U. S. Department of Justice. At the time, FBN was within the purview of the U. S. Treasury Department.

The biggest change to take effect that probably had the greatest impact was the use of electronic equipment, wiretapping, and eavesdropping, which is now legal in federal courts.

At the time of FBN, "wiretapping" was illegal. Thus, evidence obtained in federal investigations was inadmissible in federal courts. Wiretapping was legal, for the most part, only in state courts. There may have been rare exceptions, so that if it became necessary to wiretap a defendant's phone in a major investigation, it would be done in conjunction with the NYCPD who had the legal authority.

The advent of the computer age and advances in technology brought about considerable changes in the agency's manpower needs, equipment, weaponry, and overall resources. The changes in technology have produced a more efficient and effective methodology, enabling the agency to become much more efficient and professional in conducting investigations.

As the demographics changed, so did the agency's target population. In FBN times, the mob was the major source of supply for drugs. Architects of organized crime, the mob financed and controlled the drug trade while the Blacks and Hispanics were the middle men or the distributors. (Latinos were then called Hispanics; while in some areas of the country Blacks were still being called Negroes).

The cry of "Black is Beautiful" that emerged with the Civil Rights Movement did away with the term "Negro" and emphasized "Black," which eventually became what it officially is today, African-American. Moreover, the "Mob" who controlled the trade, is not as involved in drug trafficking today as they were then.

As to methodology for the collection of evidence at the time, it was obtained through ounce purchases of drugs by an undercover agent or seizures of drugs found in clandestine locations. Buying one ounce or more of heroin/cocaine from a Black or Latino drug dealer was the NORM. The price ranged from $300 to $500 per ounce, depending on the quality or grade. However, if the purchase was made from an "Italian" with mob connections or a guy who had links to the mob and he sold you an ounce of high-grade "stuff" or an ounce of "pure," then regardless of price, you had a real big quality case.

Although the standard buy was an ounce, if you anticipated buying a large quantity of drugs and you wanted a sample, you would buy a "spoon" (small bag) of heroin or cocaine. Today, DEA might purchase a small quantity of drugs or more as a sample, but its focus is on seizures of huge amounts of drugs and the development of large conspiracy cases against the drug lords of the Colombian, Mexican, or Dominican cartels. They manufacture and produce the drugs in tonnage quantities for distribution to the U.S. and other world markets.

The magnitude of the drug problem throughout the years has undoubtedly broadened DEA's scope of its enforcement efforts to include money laundering and narco-terrorism.

Money laundering, the process of making and/or using proceeds from drug crimes and corruption (dirty money), into legitimate assets (clean money), is truly a complicated and complex subject which requires a broader explanation and a more comprehensive study.

During FBN times, the mob, of course, had its own brand of money laundering through its organized crime efforts. While there's no absolute definition of narco-terrorism, there's a general understanding that it's an attempt by narcotic traffickers to influence the policies of a government or nation through violence and intimidation.

While there have been some changes within the agency, the role of the undercover agent (also referred to as the UC), as well as the informant (CI), has remained unchanged.

The UC is a law enforcement officer, a federal agent, or a detective with the police department or any law enforcement agency, who has official law enforcement credentials. The informant (CI) is usually a convicted felon who is trying to work off his case by cooperating with law enforcement in order to have his case dismissed or have the charges reduced.

Working undercover is often misunderstood, even by law enforcement officers themselves. There is a difference between real undercover work, and what is often perceived as real, but is more artificial. For instance, growing a beard and putting on a pair of sunglasses and glancing through your newspaper to conduct surveillance on a suspect in and around Macy's department store in New York City can be defined as undercover work and it is. However, it's fair to say that, by any measure, it is not the same nor does it compare to the following and more realistic scenario, for instance.

An undercover agent (UC), while portraying the role of a drug dealer, finds himself in a dilapidated building in Fort Apache in the Bronx in the wee hours of the morning in the company of a bunch of other drug dealers, all of whom are smoking pot or sniffing coke. They're all waiting for the connection (source of supply) to return with the shit (heroin/cocaine) that you bought from him a couple of hours before. As you wait for the connection, you go through some horrifying and frightening moments, as you're strongly encouraged or urged to smoke marijuana and/ or sniff cocaine while you wait. The restlessness can affect the undercover agent physically as well as psychologically. His mind is on many things, the drugs, the money and the shady and unsavory characters around him. The anticipation is that everything will turn out well, but no one has a crystal ball. Anything can happen at any given time. It seems to me that there's a distinct difference between the scenarios in Fort Apache versus the one at Macy's.

Similarly, infiltration cases can also pose a very real and dangerous situation for the undercover agent. Whether it be portraying the role of a "Wise-guy" trying to join the mob or a right-wing extremist trying to join some radical organization, the UC must divorce himself from his true persona and immerse himself totally in the role he's portraying.

After successfully infiltrating the group, the notion of "befriend and betray" could become a real issue for the UC, as he struggles with his feelings and emotions when one of the gang members he's become very friendly with, is arrested and is now awaiting trial.

In a courtroom facing jail time, the defendant's fate is predicated on his friend's (the agent's) testimony regarding the evidence obtained by his so-called friend, the agent. This certainly does not compare with the less dangerous undercover assignments.

Moreover, there are moments when the UC has to deal with heavy decision making, particularly as it pertain to crossing the very thin line that exists between legal and illegal. There are situations that may call for the undercover agent to violate the law, such as using drugs or committing burglary or theft. Needless to say, there are very strict rules and regulations governing such activities and they must be followed. Approval for activities that border on the illegal must be approved by management at the highest level.

Problems can also surface when, during the course of the investigation, someone in the community or neighborhood, especially someone who knows you well, recognizes you and then comes over and exchanges greetings like, "How are you? How are you doing/feeling? Are you still on the job?" No doubt, people are just trying to be friendly or neighborly, but while it can impugn the investigation, it can create a perilous situation for the UC.

While there are a number of issues and considerations one must take into account when working undercover, clearly not every law enforcement officer is suited for this type of activity or this kind of work.

4

Probationary Period

S hortly after being sworn in by District Supervisor George Gaffney on that fateful day in August 1960, I was assigned to Ben Fitzgerald (Group 1) who became my immediate supervisor. In addition to being my supervisor, Fitzgerald went on to become a good friend and mentor. At a time when it wasn't fashionable to have "ethnics" on board, I became one of the first few "Hispanic" agents with the agency.

Fitzgerald, or Fitz as he was called, was an attorney by profession, a bright individual, as well known for his Irish heritage and Irish wit as he was for his Roman Catholic faith. He was a gentleman and a scholar who looked more like a college professor than he did an agent. He often used the term, "The Human Element," a characteristic found in the human condition that separates the conventional from the non-conventional.

Fitz's professorial demeanor was obviously inconsistent with that of the sharp and tough street agent, in neither behavior nor speech. But to many of us, he was the father or the big brother who took the time to listen, especially when necessary.

After an exchange of greetings, we sat down and Fitz went over some of FBN's policies and procedures. Fitz reviewed some fundamental issues that he felt needed to be addressed and wanted me to be aware of, especially since I was in my probationary period. He went on to inform me that for administrative purposes, he was going to assign me to work with Frank Waters, acting group leader (Group 1), albeit I would not be working for Waters exclusively.

When asked to explain, Fitz stated that most of the agents in the office worked in teams of two or three. Thus, everyone was paired off so that no one worked alone. However, the larger issue was also the dearth of Spanish-speaking agents, not only in the office, but throughout the agency. Consequently, that would affect me more than the other agents, because I would be working with teams of agents from other groups who needed a Spanish-speaking agent to make cases.

Working predominantly in an undercover capacity, I was constantly working with informants who would bring me to the targeted drug dealer, at which time, I was expected to make purchases of drugs (heroin/cocaine) from the dealer, with as little involvement from the informant as possible. There were also requests for translation services from around the office and the Courthouse Squad, a unit assigned to the U.S. Attorney's Office, occasionally causing distractions or disruptions by taking up precious time from on-going investigations.

Fitz went on to say that the lack of Spanish-speaking agents had obviously created a problem, not just for the New York City office, but other FBN offices in Newark, Philadelphia, and Boston. Fortunately or unfortunately, I was going to be kept very busy, working frequently for other groups in the office or working with agents from other neighboring cities or towns. Fitz added that the one thing to remember was "Don't spread yourself too thin."

Fitz asked me where I was from, and when I told him I was from Brooklyn, he grinned and stated that he was also from Brooklyn, adding that "If you're from Brooklyn and you have some street smarts, you'll be okay." Fitz then brought me over and introduced me to Frank Waters, stating curiously, "Frank, this is Louie G as he's going to be called, and he's a new agent who's been assigned to our group. In fact, he's from Brooklyn, speaks Spanish fluently, and I think he's a potential dynamo. I'm assigning him to you, so look after him, provide him with some direction, and good luck."

After the usual greetings, Waters immediately asked me if I had any law enforcement experience. I said no, and he replied that although it would be helpful if I had, it won't matter because I was bilingual and, if I had some street smarts, everything would eventually fall into place. With a grin on his face, he added, "Besides, you're from Brooklyn, you're Hispanic, you look like you got some street smarts, and that counts for more than you think."

"Our biggest problem," he said flatly, "is going to be keeping you from being overused by agents from the other groups who want to use you to make buys for them, but there's not much we can do about that. In the meantime, I'm going to give you some photos of fugitives and suspected drug dealers, okay. Look at them, and let me know if you know or recognize anyone."

I went through the pictures, which was something like a "Rogue's Gallery" without recognizing anyone except for one, Jose Centeno, formerly a member of the "Mambo Aces," a precision dance team that put on exhibitions at the Palladium Ballroom in midtown Manhattan. The Palladium was, at that time, a dance club known as the home of Latin Music, where some of the best Latin bands or orchestras played and professional dance teams performed.

As time went by, both Fitzgerald and Waters were accurate with their assessment of my role during that probationary period. It wasn't long before Agents Smith and Dower from Group 3 came knocking at the door and asked me to help them out. They had a Hispanic informant they wanted me to work with so they could make cases on several dealers from "El Barrio" (Spanish Harlem) and the South Bronx. I began working with Agents Smith and

Dower, and together we proceeded on a mission where we made a multitude of good cases for their group.

The first year was going very smoothly as I succeeded in making a good number of cases with different agents from different groups. I became acquainted with some of the more well-known violators throughout the city, the Angelet Brothers, (George and Willie), William (Cockeyed Willie) Rivera, John (Johnny Moonface) Montanes, Bumpy Johnson and Anthony (Baby Face) Morelli. As I approached the end of my first year on the job, I was learning very quickly about the illegal drug trade, the drug dealers, their modus operandi (MO) and the jargon of a drug culture that had its own lexicon.

At the same time, it had also become clear that being one of the very few Latino Agents, I was also being over-utilized. Sometimes it felt that perhaps I was being abused; but if it did appear that way, it certainly was not by design. I certainly didn't see it that way. I thought the hard work was beginning to pay off, not only for myself, but the agents I was working with and the agency in general.

A journey man agent was expected to make (two-three) cases a month. I was averaging five or six cases per month and ordinarily that would be a good thing. But, it was really bitter-sweet as it caused me to fall behind on my paperwork. There were standard daily and monthly reports required. Investigative reports were also required and depending on the type of case, they were often voluminous in content.

While I was probably going too fast too soon, it didn't matter. I just wanted to prove that I could compete with the best. Furthermore, I was young, industrious, and willing to learn every-thing there was to learn. I couldn't care less about anything else. Needless to say, I was enthusiastic and determined to succeed, so I was not about to complain nor was I going to raise any issues. I was just trying to show everyone that I was good at what I did and

I belonged. Despite the lack of formal training, I was doing rather well during the probationary period.

However there was a price to be paid for being the only game in town. I rarely went home early since most of the work was during the evening hours. The volume of paperwork and the tendency to fall behind proved to be a nightmare. The issue itself would later come back to haunt me.

As to formal training for agents, it was FBN policy that new agents, after being sworn in, or by the end of their probationary period, were required to attend the Treasury Enforcement Law Officers Training School, or TELOTS, as it was called.

The school consisted of eight weeks' mandatory indoor/outdoor training. It was the equivalent of today's 'ACADEMY' for rookie law enforcement officers at the local or federal level. Here I was, about to complete my probationary period, and I had not yet received any formal training. Fitz expressed concern over the issue and told me to slow down on making cases as he was in the process of having my name assigned for the next class to attend TELOTS. Fitz said that the only training I was receiving was "on the job" training. While that was great experience, attendance at TELOTS was essential. Fitz instructed me not to make any more cases until he said so, and he told me that he'd made plans for me to be registered in the next class. True to his word, the next day I received notice to report to the school by the following weekend.

5

The Gennaro Salzano Investigation

A s I sat at my desk, preparing for my trip to Washington to attend school, a colleague from another group, Patty Biase, came by to talk to me. We had a brief conversation during which time he showed me a picture of a convicted drug dealer named Gennaro Salzano.

Biase asked me if I knew of him or if I had heard of him, and I said no. I asked him if I should have heard of Salzano and why he was interested in this guy. Biase told me that Salzano was a second offender and a major narcotics violator from the Italian section of Harlem who had ties to the mob. Salzano was back in the streets again dealing drugs, and Biase was anxious and eager to build a case against him.

My colleague stated that he was facing a dilemma and that I might be able to help him out. I indicated that I would be glad to help him, but I had been instructed to stop making any more cases, as I was scheduled to go to school in Washington D. C. by the end of the week. I told Biase that I would be glad to help him out upon my return from Washington.

Biase explained that he couldn't wait that long. He needed an undercover agent to make a buy from Salzano as soon as possible. He was having problems with an informant who was reluctant to bring just anyone to Salzano. Biase had spoken to a couple of other UC agents, but the informant had declined to bring anyone of them to Salzano. Biase added that all he wanted was for me to make the initial purchase. We could resume further negotiations with Salzano upon my return from school.

I told Biase to speak to Fitz, and if he approved, I'd be more than happy to do it.

Biase left to speak with Fitz, and a short time later returned and said that Fitz had agreed to my helping him, provided that we kept initial activities to a minimum. Fitz cited, as an example, that we should control the situation by making the first buy from the suspect and not making arrangements for further purchases until I finished school. Fitz's main concern was not to allow the investigation to be dragged out during the initial purchase, since that would lead to my missing the upcoming class. I told Biase that since Fitz had approved, let's do it.

Biase let me know that his informant had been reluctant to bring anyone to Salzano because Salzano was very "hinky" (apprehensive) about doing business with anyone outside of his close circle of friends. When I questioned him as to what made him think that the informant would bring me to Salzano, Biase said that he was aware of the work I had been doing with Smith and Dower from his group as well as Schrier and Selvaggi.

He had made inquiries about me, had received good reports, and therefore wanted to go forward with the plan. Besides, I was a new face, I didn't look like a cop, and I was Hispanic. Biase went on to say that there was no specific criterion for success, but he felt fairly confident that the plan might work.

Biase clearly stated that Salzano had ties to the mob, dealt in large quantities of drugs and he was hungry for money. Moreover, he suggested that if the informant succeeded in bringing me in, he wanted me to buy at least a few ounces or possibly 1/8th of a kilo from Salzano. He also stated that when I returned from school, we'd consider buying more to develop the case. I agreed and then went to meet the informant who was in an adjoining room by Biase's office.

Biase indicated that the informant's name was Freddie Truppa, a convicted felon himself, who was trying to help his own cause by assisting FBN in making cases against other drug dealers. Truppa was friends with Salzano but, as mentioned, he'd been very apprehensive and extremely reluctant in bringing anyone to Salzano. According to Truppa, Salzano was a very suspicious guy who did not trust anyone nor would he deal with anyone outside of his own circle of friends. In fact, Salzano had always been unapproachable. Furthermore, Salzano had a bad temper and was a dangerous individual. If he ever found out he'd been set up, he'd have you killed or he'd kill you himself. Well aware of Salzano's reputation, Truppa refused to bring anyone to him.

I informed Biase that it seemed like a strong case and I would be glad to help. But as he himself indicated, Truppa refused to bring anyone to Salzano, so what made Truppa think that Salzano would be willing to meet me, much less talk and negotiate a drug deal? Biase pointed out that having worked undercover on many cases himself, he'd considered going with Truppa to meet Salzano and making the case himself. But Truppa, concerned for his own safety, was adamant and would not, under any circumstances, consider bringing anyone, including Biase, to Salzano. However, Biase reiterated what he'd said earlier, that being "Hispanic" and a fresh new face, might do the trick, so I said, "Let's go give it a try."

Upon entering the room, I met Truppa, and after an exchange of greetings, we had a brief conversation. Truppa asked me a few questions concerning my real name, my undercover name, where I was from, and where I grew up, etc. I provided him with some background information and told him that I used different undercover names such as Ango, Bobby Bright Eyes, and the most recent, Bobby Cubano. Truppa then asked me what was my nationality, and I said, "Puerto Rican," to which Truppa responded, "Wow, you don't look Puerto Rican."

"Why? What difference does that make? Do you have a problem with that?"

"No," he replied, "but Gennaro might."

"Why is that?" I asked.

Truppa said he didn't know, but Gennaro was always complaining about the "Spics" moving into the neighborhood.

"Really?" I said, "Well, that's what I am, and there's not much we can do about I. Meanwhile, you can tell Salzano that this has nothing to do with housing. This is all about business and making money. In fact, tell him anything you want. After all, you just said that I don't look Puerto Rican, correct? Well, then, tell him whatever you think I look like—Italian, Irish, Jewish. Tell him whatever you're comfortable with. But just make sure that whatever you tell him, you let me know so that we're both on the same page."

Truppa said, "You're right. If the issue comes up, you're Bobby Cubano from Miami, and you're half Italian and half Spanish. Is that okay with you?"

I replied, "Yeah, that's fine."

Truppa seemed resentful of having brought up the ethnicity issue, but I told him to forget it. He felt a bit more comfortable but was still apprehensive about bringing anyone to Salzano.

Truppa repeated his reason for being so overly cautious was that Salzano had recently gotten out of jail, was very suspicious and very dangerous. Truppa reiterated that if Salzano found out that he'd been set up he would not hesitate to kill you or both of us. I told Truppa that I understood and sympathized with his situation, but if we were going to make the case, we needed to work together and try to simplify things. Truppa agreed, and by this time, we had begun to feel comfortable with each other. Truppa now seemed a bit less anxious and said to Biase, "I like this guy. Let's give it a shot."

Biase asked Truppa how much Salzano wanted for an ounce of heroin, and Truppa said the price varied between $400 and

$600. However, Truppa strongly urged that we consider buying more than a couple of ounces because despite the fact that Salzano was hinky, the money would certainly appeal to him and whet his appetite. Biase reminded Truppa that if we were going to buy larger quantities, we better be talking about high-grade stuff, to which Truppa replied that the more we bought, the better the quality and price. Truppa quickly suggested that, for starters, we buy a quarter kilo and then follow that up with the idea that he, not me, should make the initial buy.

Questioned as to why such a large quantity for a first buy, Truppa replied that Salzano would feel much more comfortable dealing with him rather than me, particularly the first time around. Furthermore, despite his reluctance and apprehension, the more money he saw, the more eager he would be to do business.

Biase and I looked at each other, excused ourselves, and then left the room for a brief private conversation. We both seemed concerned about the same thing. I said, "Look, he's your informant, so you know the guy better than I do, but I think he's up to something. I think he's got his own agenda. He continues to talk about Salzano's reluctance and apprehension about meeting anyone, and suddenly we're talking about the purchase of a quarter kilo. Furthermore, he's now willing to bring me in, but wants to make the buy himself, so what does he want me there for? Observation purposes? I don't like it, and I'm concerned because I think he's got something up his sleeve,"

Biase said "You're right. I don't know what the fuck he's up to, but we'll soon find out. But, don't worry about it, you call the shots. You're in charge. I trust you and your instincts. Use your discretion, but be very careful and keep your eye on both of these bastards."

"If anything is going down that you don't like, or you smell a rat, call the whole thing off, get the fuck out of there, and try to get back to us as soon as you can. It's not going to be his way.

It's going to be our way. I'll get approval for the money and the amount we're going to buy, and you take care of the undercover scenarios as they play out."

We went back to Truppa and Biase said to him, "Look, we got approval to buy four ounces, which is slightly less than an eighth of a kilo, okay. But Louie's in charge and will make that decision depending on how negotiations go. More important however, we can't have you make the buy for fear of entrapment, so Louie will make the buy, understood?" Truppa grudgingly nodded in agreement.

We made it clear to Truppa that if the "stuff" turned out to be top quality, the next time we'd consider buying a quarter kilo. But I told him, "One step at a time, okay? And remember, you're in no position to dictate or set terms. Louie will run the show, and you have to go along with what he says. Otherwise, it's no deal. Understand? Meanwhile, why don't you two get together on your story and make arrangements as to when and where to meet and so on."

I was excited. This was a case with real potential and being in charge only served to whet my appetite to get on with this new adventure.

6

Meeting Salzano

On May 1, 1961, during the mid-afternoon hours, Truppa and I, along with Biase and other agents from Biase's group (Jack Brady and Jimmy O'Connell) met in the vicinity of East 113 Street and East River Drive in Manhattan to discuss a planned strategy.

The plan was for me to meet Salzano at Truppa's apartment and then negotiate and purchase, if possible, one-eighth of a kilo or at the very least four ounces of heroin from Salzano for sixteen hundred dollars. Furthermore, because the meeting was going to be at Truppa's apartment it was important, to the extent possible, to have Truppa say as little as possible and not get involved in the negotiations for fear of entrapment. The idea was to let me do most of the talking and negotiating. Truppa was nervous and uncertain often reminding us that Salzano was very cautious, and, if he suspected anything, he wouldn't go through with the deal. I told Truppa not to worry and leave things up to me. The following day, late in the afternoon, I proceeded to Truppa's residence under the surveillance of Agents Biase, Brady, and O'Connell.

I entered Truppa's apartment, and after a quick exchange of greetings, Truppa, who was in the apartment alone, said that Salzano had been there waiting for me, but then decided to go to a local club and wait for us there. I told Truppa to go to the club and tell him that I had arrived. Truppa left the apartment to meet Salzano.

A short time later, Truppa returned alone, but indicated that Salzano was on his way. Shortly thereafter, Salzano arrived, and Truppa introduced me as "Bobby Cubano," a friend of his from New York and Miami. We exchanged greetings, but Salzano, a tough-looking Italian with a ruddy complexion, was very quiet, seemed reluctant to talk, and appeared to be somewhat apprehensive. When it became apparent that he wasn't going to say much, I broke the ice and began the conversation. "Look," I said, "I'll get right to the point. I'm from Brooklyn, but I travel a lot between here and Miami. I have a good customer base in both places, and I also have a couple of guys I cop [buy] from. But the shit I've been getting lately is really bad because it's weak. When you get weak stuff and then cut it some more, the stuff you're putting out on the street is not good. And if that continues, you slowly begin to lose your customers and that's not good for business."

"Now Freddie here tells me you've got some good quality stuff. If the stuff is that good or better than what I've been getting, then I'll be back for more. A kilo or more, and we could have a healthy business relationship. In fact, if it's that good, I'll buy a lot more weight. But first, let's talk about what we can do now. What kind of stuff do you have, and what's it gonna cost?"

Salzano answered with a question of his own. "First of all, before we do anything, where do you know Freddie from?"

I said, "It was some time ago, in the Criminal Court Building downtown Manhattan on Center Street. I was in court talking to my lawyer who was trying to work out a plea bargain for me. I had an argument with my girlfriend that escalated into a nasty altercation. She called the police and told them I slapped her, which was not true. I was arrested for simple assault, but she didn't show up at court, so the charges were dropped. My attorney said that he could have the assault charge dismissed, but I would have to plead guilty to a disorderly conduct, which I did. Freddie was in court for a case of his own, but it looked like we had a few things in common."

At this time, I walked over to Truppa and said to him, "Remember, Freddie?" And Freddie replied, "Yeah, that's right, except you had better luck than I did."

"Since we got along, we continued to talk, then went out for a couple of drinks and slowly became acquainted. We saw each other a few more times in court, and since we'd both been involved with drugs, we agreed to stay in touch and help each other in future deals."

Truppa, who seemed to get the idea of where I was going with the conversation, interjected, "Yeah, you're right, but you had a better lawyer. You got a good deal, but I got fucked."

I explained to Salzano the problem I was having in getting quality stuff. "I continued to get bad shit, and that's why I was looking for a new connection. I recently called Freddie, and he said you could probably help me out, so here we are. I could ask you a few questions, but I won't. I'll take Freddie's word about you and your reputation. But, let's get this straight my man, I'm not gonna sit here and bullshit for hours and then walk away empty-handed. So, if you are not gonna help me, or you don't want to do business with me, let me know and I'll go somewhere else."

Salzano, no longer taciturn, began to open up and stated that he'd recently gotten out of jail and he had to be very careful and cautious with whom he dealt. I told him that I understood the situation, and if I were in his place, I would do the same thing.

Salzano asked me how much I was looking to (cop) buy, and I told him that I was looking to buy an eighth of a kilo, but since this was our first time doing business, I would take four ounces. Salzano stated that he could get me four ounces for $2,000. I told him the price was too high, and then asked him if he could lower the price.

Salzano replied that the stuff was dynamite and I was going to be very happy because the stuff was pure; I would be able to cut it several times and double or possibly triple my money. I told him that I wanted to make certain that the stuff was as good as he claimed and, if it was, I'd be back for more. I also said that if he gave me a good price on the four pieces, I would return and buy a quarter kilo or more. Salzano went on to say that he'd let me have the four pieces for $1,800, emphasizing that the stuff was really pure horse [heroin]. We haggled over price, but Salzano wouldn't budge.

Realizing that we had reached somewhat of a stalemate, I told him that since I did not have enough money for the four, I would settle for three instead. Salzano grudgingly replied that he would give me the four pieces for $1,600 and I could pay him the balance of $200 when I returned. Salzano further stated that he was so confident that I would be satisfied with the stuff that I would return to buy more at which time he would add the $200 I owed him to the price of the quarter kilo or whatever amount I would buy. I thanked him for letting me have the four ounces, but made it clear that I could settle for three. Salzano, who by this time was anxious to get the deal over and done with, stated that his connection dealt in large quantities of horse and he didn't want to upset the apple cart, so it was best for me to take the four pieces and leave well enough alone.

Salzano added that by doing so, everyone would be satisfied, which made for a good beginning. Salzano then asked me for the money, at which time I told him that I would take the four ounces but I wasn't going to front the money. I asked him to go get the stuff and I would wait in the apartment or anywhere he wanted me to wait. Salzano immediately stated that under no circumstances could he get the stuff without the money. His connection was a big guy with mob ties and there was no screwing around. That's the way he did business. Salzano then made it quite clear that if I didn't give him the money, there was no deal, pure and simple.

At the time, it was FBN policy not to front monies on drug buys lest you get beat for the money. If that happened, then the agents on the case would be responsible for the money and it would come out of their own pocket. However, it was something that was not etched in stone, as the decision was usually left to the discretion of the undercover agent. Thus, it was my decision, although I had not yet been faced with that type of decision previously. Salzano had been talking quite a bit and, unaccustomed as he was to talking, by this time we had become fairly comfortable with each other. I felt I had gained Salzano's confidence enough that he would return with the stuff and not abscond with the money.

Furthermore, I was going to wait for him at Truppa's apartment, and if he didn't come back, Truppa would have a lot of answering to do and there would be hell to pay. Undercover agents, more often than not, rely and trust their instincts and gut feeling. I felt that I'd reached that level, and therefore I gave him the money up front.

I counted out $1,600 of official government funds and gave it to Salzano. He counted the money again and said he'd be back in about an hour. I immediately went to the nearest telephone booth in the area and called the base station at headquarters and left a message for Biase and the agents on surveillance that everything was going according to plan and that Salzano had left to go meet his connection and get the stuff. Both Truppa and I returned to the apartment and approximately fifteen minutes later, Salzano returned and stated that he had telephoned someone and arrangements were made to pick up the stuff at 6:00 that evening. Salzano gave me the money back, saying he didn't want to keep me waiting more than I had to.

At approximately 5:30 p.m., Salzano said he was ready to

leave and I told him that I would like to go along with him. I also told Salzano that if the stuff was as powerful as he indicated, I would make it worthwhile for him the next time because I would not just take a quarter kilo, but I would take one kilo and throw him an extra $100 cash if he took me to his connection.

Salzano quickly retorted, "Whoa, pal, we're just getting acquainted. I like you, and I've taken you into my confidence, something I never do. This is the first time we do business, and you already want to meet the man? Well, the man doesn't want to meet you. Understand?"

I then said, "Look, I'm going to be buying a lot of stuff from you for a lot of bread, so the least you can do is let me go with you and meet the man."

Salzano replied, "Listen, pal, you got lucky today cause I don't deal with outsiders. But, you're a nice cat and Freddie says you're okay, so I'll tell you what. You can come with me, but you're not going to meet the man. You understand? I'll tell you where to wait for me."

I agreed, and we left the apartment and went to East 116th Street and 2nd Avenue where we hailed a cab. The cab took us to West 75th Street and Broadway where we entered a bar located at the southeast corner. Salzano asked for the money, and we went into the bathroom where I gave him the $1,600. Salzano told me to have a drink and wait for him by the bar as he wouldn't be gone long.

Approximately fifteen minutes later, Salzano returned to the bar and placed a newspaper on the counter. He told me that the stuff was in a black paper bag underneath the newspaper. Salzano said that I'd be very satisfied with the horse because it was pure shit and it was dynamite. I thanked him for giving me a break on the price and asked him where I could contact him for future purchases. Salzano said that for the time being I should go through Truppa. Salzano then quickly left the premises.

Upon leaving the bar, I immediately looked underneath the newspaper and opened the black bag and noticed a cellophane package containing a white powder. I went directly to the bathroom where I field-tested the white powder.

To test the drugs, undercover agents would normally carry a small vial containing sulfuric acid and some other chemical solution. If the contents turned purple the test was positive for heroin. Any other color, the test was negative which meant you got something other than heroin, possibly 'milk sugar.' I broke the vial in half, cut through the cellophane package and poured a tiny portion of the powder into the vial. The test was positive for heroin as the powder turned purple.

Approximately one hour later all the agents involved in the case met at the office. The white powder was retested and found to be positive. The evidence was initialed by all concerned and routinely prepared in accordance with the chain of custody. The evidence was secured by Agent O'Connell and quickly sent to the U.S. Chemist's Office for official testing and analysis.

Biase thanked me for a job well done and informed me that after receiving the first call, they followed Salzano to some location in midtown Manhattan, but after an hour on surveillance, Salzano did not re-appear and they discontinued surveillance. They had not yet determined who the source of supply was but they would continue their surveillance on Salzano. He was also confident it would be only a matter of time before they would ascertain who the source might be.

I reminded Biase that I was leaving for school within the next few days and would not return for almost two months. Therefore, it was essential that Truppa go back as soon as possible to speak with Salzano and tell him that I was going to Miami but would be back within a month or two. Biase agreed and Truppa indicated that he'd go and talk to Salzano as soon as he could.

I had worked very hard during my probationary period and I looked forward to going to school and getting the formal training required of all agents. At the same time, I also welcomed a break from the grueling pace and since I had yet received any formal training, I was looking forward to it.

7

Reality Check

U pon arrival in Washington, I checked in at the hotel where I was staying and reviewed the school schedule for the week. All indications were that there would be classroom work in the morning and fieldwork in the afternoon. Nonetheless, I was still looking forward to the school and some formal training.

The following morning, I got up early and went to have breakfast at a local coffee shop. I bought a New York newspaper, and as soon as I picked up the paper, I saw the headline in heavy black print that read in effect: "Drug Dealer slain – Body dumped in Bronx Lot." I couldn't believe what I was reading.

A quick review of the article indicated that Freddie Truppa, the informant I had worked with, had been murdered by his associate, another drug dealer named Gennaro Salzano over the proceeds of a drug deal. Truppa's body had been wrapped up in a blanket and was dumped in a vacant lot in the Bronx. Two men were being held for the slaying, Salzano and his brother-in-law, whom I had not met.

I was in a state of shock. I couldn't believe what I was reading. It was like a nightmare. Truppa had introduced me to Salzano and I bought approximately four ounces of heroin from the guy. It was a good case and everything seemed fine. Salzano and I had parted company in good terms, and Truppa had not even been involved. Because I had to be away for some time, Truppa was sent to meet with him and explain that I would return in a couple of months. And now I am learning that Salzano murdered Truppa. What happened? This was unbelievable, it was bizarre. If I had been with Truppa, would Salzano have killed me as well? Many things went through my mind, all nerve racking and disconcerting.

On the one hand, I was quite excited because it was a very good case that presented me with a challenge. I was a young rookie with only nine months on the job as a narcotic agent, and I had made a case against a major violator. It was a case with a lot of potential yet to be developed. Conversely, I also could have been killed. *What happened? What went wrong?*

I realized that I was supposed to go back to Salzano with Truppa to buy larger quantities of drugs, but obviously I had to attend school. For a brief spell I thought to myself if I had gone along with Truppa I could have been killed.

I kept reading, looking for additional and more specific information. I bought a couple of other newspapers but found none. All the newspapers said basically the same thing, that Salzano killed Truppa after a heated dispute over the proceeds of drug sales.

This was rather interesting, because I remembered that when I initially met Truppa, there was a moment during our initial conversation when he attempted to change our game plan by trying to increase the quantity and the price of the drugs.

This had immediately raised red flags for me. Both Biase and I had expressed concern over Truppa's overture, so it certainly was not beyond the realm of possibility that Truppa would try to pull a fast one on Salzano. Although this seemed unlikely, Salzano was known to be dangerous enough to kill anyone who messed with him. Whatever the reason, an angered Salzano shot Truppa in the head, killing him instantly. He then wrapped the body up in blankets, and drove to a vacant lot on Bruckner Boulevard and White Plains Road in the Bronx where he dumped the body.

He was a vicious and cold-blooded murderer who didn't think twice about killing someone, much less a business partner or a friend. I asked myself a whole slew of questions with seemingly no right or wrong answers. But I couldn't avoid the much larger question, the one that I struggled with for some time. If I had been with Truppa, would Salzano have killed me too? Regardless, I considered myself fortunate to be alive, and I was very happy to be attending school. Nonetheless I was shocked by what I was reading, but unfortunately, I would have to wait until I got a break during school hours to call the New York office to get the update from Biase or any of the other guys involved in the case.

On the very first day of school during a break period, I called the office and spoke to Biase, who confirmed what I had read. Biase went on to say that they were working on the case with detectives from the NYPD and that Salzano and his brother-in-law had been arrested, but the brother-in-law had been released. Biase also said that I was very lucky not to have been there.

His feeling was that if I had gone back with Truppa to see Salzano, Lord knows what could have happened. Given Salzano's record and reputation, there was little doubt that I could have also been a victim. When I asked Biase if there were any specifics as to why Salzano killed Truppa, Biase said that it remained unclear.

The newspapers had indicated that it was over how much money each would get from the proceeds of previous drug deals. There was also speculation that someone in the area may have recognized me as an agent and then "blew the whistle" for a price, telling Salzano that he'd sold to an undercover agent. And there was also a possibility that it could have been another informant who recognized me from the court or someone who had it in for Truppa. There was even some talk of the possibility of a crooked or corrupt cop who might have seen me in court and wanted to cash in. It was all speculation, but Biase felt they would soon have an answer. They were working on the case in conjunction with detectives from the NYC police Department and he was confident they would soon have an answer.

In retrospect, I thought of the initial meeting between Biase, Truppa, and myself before I met Salzano. We had been discussing prices and amounts of drugs to purchase when suddenly Truppa began to inquire about buying a larger amount for more money. Both Biase and I became concerned and suspicious as to Truppa having his own agenda. However, we had set him straight about what we wanted to do and the case was moving along as planned until the homicide.

Clearly, the issue of money is always major in drug deals, and this one was no different. Biase indicated that Salzano was in state prison pending forthcoming hearings and arraignment on the murder charge. But, he wasn't sure what action, if any, the U.S. Attorney's Office would take on our case, since it was a "one buy" case which can be problematic for the government because of the entrapment issue.

The priority was on the homicide which was a state case. At some point down the road the U.S. Attorney's Office would determine what they were going to do with the federal drug case. In either case, we would be notified.

Biase thanked me for a job well done and indicated that my role on the case was over, except perhaps to testify in court if the case went to trial. He told me to enjoy myself at school and hopefully by the time I returned, there might be some new information from the U.S. Attorney's Office. Biase went on to say that while my role was over in the case, he would like to use me in future investigations, but there was time to discuss that later.

8

The Trial

U pon finishing school, I returned home. While I satisfied the academic requirements, my mind was continually reviewing all the fieldwork, the homicide and the thought that I could easily have been a victim was constantly on my mind. Admittedly, the fieldwork (pistol range; Judo instruction; technical projects and undercover/surveillance assignments) enabled me to better cope. Although I did well scholastically, I was better at fieldwork. I was particularly proud of the fact that on a memorization project where one had to match baby photos of celebrities with photos of them as adults, I was the only one in class who got them all correct.

Shortly after returning to duty, Salzano's case for the murder came up in state court, and we learned that he would not be charged with first degree murder because no murder weapon was found. After killing Truppa, Salzano had thrown the gun into the East River (near his home) and without the murder weapon, the state could only charge him with manslaughter. When the case came up for trial, Salzano plead guilty to the manslaughter charge and was sentenced to seven to fourteen (7–14) years in state prison.

Although our case against Salzano was a one-buy case, which is often difficult to prosecute, the U.S. Attorney's Office for the Southern District of New York decided to move forward with the federal case and try Salzano anyway.

The Assistant U. S. Attorney assigned to the case then called me in for a pre-trial hearing. We met at his office, during which time he made it clear that Salzano was an undesirable individual with ties to the mob and as a second offender, he belonged in jail. Therefore, he was moving forward with the trial. 'One buy' cases were difficult to prosecute for fear of entrapment. The Informant who brought me to Salzano was now dead, creating an additional problem. Nevertheless, the government proceeded to go to trial and hopefully convict Salzano on the sales charge.

The AUSA (Ass't U. S. Attorney) was very much aware that Salzano was doing 7 to 14 years in state prison for manslaughter instead of the murder. He was anxious to try Salzano because a conviction in federal court would mean that Salzano, as a second offender, would get a minimum of 10 years. Furthermore, the AUSA would seek to have Salzano serve the sentence consecutively and not concurrently.

The AUSA believed that Salzano's defense would be "Mistaken Identity" since the informant was no longer around. Moreover, he figured that Salzano would deny the incident ever took place and that he'd never met me before. In the final analysis, it would be his word against mine. The AUSA also realized that it was quite possible for the government to lose the case due to the entrapment issue. He was emphatic in telling me to refresh my memory and be prepared, as the trial was imminent, and we were going to do some serious ass-kicking.

Several weeks later, the AUSA called me at the office to inform me that the defense attorney for Salzano had filed a motion to suppress the evidence in the case, and it had been granted by the court. The motion was fair and legal and the defense was starting off on the right foot, but it made the AUSA a bit more aware and aggressive.

Basically, granting of the motion meant that under no circumstances could the government, during the trial, disclose or allude to the fact that Salzano was serving time in state prison for the murder of Truppa, as this would be biased and prejudicial to the defendant. Given that scenario, the trial would certainly come down to Gennaro's word against mine and mistaken identity seemed as the appropriate defense.

Subsequently, the trial began at the U.S. courthouse in lower Manhattan and the jurors were selected with Judge Edward Weinfeld, presiding. Salzano was obviously sitting at the defense table with his attorney. When called to testify, I took the stand and as I looked straight at Salzano, I noticed that his appearance had changed slightly; he had grown a mustache and his hair was much longer. His ruddy complexion had vanished, but his scornful and sinister looks remained the same. His overall appearance was that of the evil villain in a cowboy movie. But, he was still the same Gennaro Salzano that I bought the drugs from.

The defense had one witness, and that was Salzano. The government, on the other hand, had my direct testimony to refute Salzano's assertions of innocence and corroborating testimony by having the agent(s) on surveillance testify. It also introduced physical evidence in the form of the four envelopes containing the heroin that I purchased from Salzano.

The glassine envelopes were initialed by all the agents involved in the case and, in accordance with the chain of custody, the evidence had been adequately prepared, secured, and had been submitted to the U. S. Chemist's Office for safekeeping.

In addition to my report explaining what had taken place, the government also had the report of the agents on surveillance to corroborate my testimony. They would also testify about their surveillance activities on Salzano after he left the apartment to go get the drugs.

Additional evidence was presented by the government as it produced the U. S. Chemist's Report, as well as testimony by the US. Chemist confirming the quality and purity of the heroin.

The AUSA indicated that he couldn't conceive what possible defense Salzano's attorney had in mind other than mistaken identity. Moreover, despite the fact that it was a one-buy case, the preponderance of the evidence was so overwhelming that all efforts and maneuvering by the defense was unsuccessful. The defense tried to intensify cross-examination with some acute questions, but they were met with negative results. Both sides continued the trial with their respective strategy and finally it was time to sum up the case. Shortly after their summations, the jury got the case and it did not take them very long to return with a guilty verdict.

At this time, Judge Weinfeld, well-known for his flexibility, usually in favor of the defendant(s), addressed the jury and gave them a brief and unexpected speech. The Judge informed them that judges normally thanked jurors for giving up their personal time and serving as jurors. The judge made it clear that he did not adhere to that practice because he honestly and sincerely felt it was people's civic duty to serve as jurors, regardless. However, in this particular case, he said he was making an exception because they, as jurors, had indeed rendered the proper verdict without the knowledge of a particular item or very important issue in the case. The judge then told the jurors that the defendant in the case (Salzano), was presently serving time in state prison for having murdered the informant Freddie Truppa.

The Judge went on and made it clear that before the trial began, the defense had filed a motion to suppress the evidence in the case and the motion had been granted. But, they as jurors, had no knowledge of that. The judge further explained that under the law, the government could not disclose or allude to the homicide in this case; as such information would have been prejudicial to the defendant. This obviously made the case much more difficult for the prosecution, but the government did a very good job.

He added that despite not knowing that a motion had been

granted, the jurors had nevertheless rendered the proper verdict in the case and for that, he felt an obligation to thank them. The jurors, who appeared to feel good about themselves after the judge's remarks, said they were intrigued by the case, and then made a request to meet with the agents personally.

They were curious about a few things and wanted to ask the agents a few questions of their own.

The request was granted, and the jurors were escorted to the witness room where the AUSA, Agent O'Connell and I, were waiting and having a discussion. The AUSA had thanked us for a job well done, and when the jurors arrived, we exchanged greetings and then answered some of their questions. They asked some very fundamental questions about undercover work and the dangers involved. For instance, as an UC carrying a gun on undercover assignments, where specifically do we secure the weapon? In addition, do we psyche ourselves up when we're getting ready to portray a particular role? They also wanted to see how the field test was conducted to determine if the stuff we purchased was indeed heroin.

My friend and colleague Jim O'Connell was asked about surveillance techniques and what to look for during the surveillance. He was also asked how agents handle distractions or impromptu interference that occurs during the course of the investigation, especially during the purchase. It was a strange and unexpected interlude, but I enjoyed it in some ways. After answering their questions, the Jurors left the courthouse and we returned to the office.

At the time of sentencing in federal court, Salzano was sentenced to 10 years in prison, to run consecutively with his state sentence, which meant that upon completion of his state sentence of (7–14) years, he would have to serve another 10 years which was exactly what the U. S. Attorney's Office was seeking.

It had been a very interesting case that provided me with a lot of insight and experience. It had been a solid beginning for a young agent who had just completed his probationary period and was on his way supposedly to a promising future.

9

Words of Wisdom

Shortly after the Salzano investigation, Fitz called me into his office and, as a friend and mentor, said to me, "Angel Louis Gonzalez, as my mother (God rest her soul) would have called you—by your real name—listen to me carefully, young man. When you first got here, I introduced you as Louie G, a potential dynamo, and from what I've seen or witnessed thus far, I'm inclined to believe that my perception was accurate. Now, I would like you to ponder what I'm about to tell you. Do you understand?"

"Yes, Sir," I replied. "I'm listening, go on."

Fitz stated, "It's a very simple and catchy phrase that I believe you will soon come to grips with, my friend. And that is, BIG CASES, BIG PROBLEMS - LITTLE CASES, LITTLE PROBLEMS - NO CASES, NO PROBLEMS. Do you understand what I mean by that?"

I responded by repeating the phrase as I heard it. "It means literally or exactly what you said, big cases make for big problems, small cases have small problems and no cases mean no problems, etc."

Fitz quickly stated, "You're right, Angel Louie. There's no secrecy or mystery to what I said. Just be careful, because the bigger the case, the more problems you're going to have. Little cases, obviously present smaller problems, and as to no cases, no problems. But remember this, there are some people on this job that never made a case and went on to retire with a healthy pension. That's not something new to law enforcement or any other organization for that matter. It's the nature of the beast."

"However, let me also be clear. I want to emphasize that it is not the norm. Most agents are truly conscientious and dedicated individuals. But, there's always a few who are wannabes or a few others who've made it a practice of hanging by their partner's coattails. By the same token we've also had our share of role models, and there are many of those. Nevertheless, you're on the right path, Amigo, but be careful, don't go too fast. Everything in moderation."

I asked Fitz why he was telling me all this and he said because he remembered the pace I was going before I left for school. As was his style, his reply was straightforward.

"You're extremely conscientious and a very dedicated young man. And while those are very fine qualities to have, they can also work against you."

Fitz went on, "Now that you're back from school, my guess is that the pace will pick up again and being the type of person that you are, you will not let up and resume your activities at the same pace. You must understand, but also make them understand," as he pointed toward the offices beyond his desk, "that there are limitations. This agency was here before we arrived, and it will be here long after we depart. All I'm saying is slow down. Everything in moderation my friend, so slow down, okay. I remember telling you from the outset about the lack of Spanish-speaking agents throughout this agency, and since you're fully bilingual, and you're a sharp kid who's willing to help his brother agents, you're on the hot seat. Everyone wants to use you and you're always ready to comply."

My friend's serious tenor got my immediate attention.

"Every agent on this job wants to make cases, and you're in a position to facilitate that process and help them out because you're fully bilingual, you work very hard, and you're an amenable person. As a result, you'll frequently find yourself in very interesting and unique situations. You're an asset to the agency, but you're also vulnerable to being over-utilized and possibly abused, albeit not intentionally. Continue to work hard my friend, but remember what I said about BIG CASES, BIG PROBLEMS, etc. Be selective and be alert, but be careful and cautious my friend." There was no missing the seriousness of his message.

Fitz continued, "Now, as you may recall, just before you left for school, I gave permission for you to assist Biase in the initiation of the Salzano case. And that's fine because that was a real good case and you did a fine job. And thank God, you were in school when Truppa met with Salzano. Only the good Lord knows what could have happened if you had been there. But now I'm assigning you to work with Frank Waters who's working on a much bigger case for our group, and that will take priority. The case is an international investigation, a conspiracy case involving a couple of Frenchmen and a couple of mobsters in NYC.

It's a joint effort between the NYCPD–SIU, led by Detectives Egan and Grosso, and the FBN group led by Waters. Remember those names, they're important believe me."

"Naturally, you'll continue with your undercover work with other agents, but you'll also be working with Frank on this case which will require for you to work periodically with Egan, Grosso, and other detectives from SIU. But, remember what I said. Don't spread yourself so thin you begin to wear yourself out and inadvertently create problems for yourself. So be aware and be careful, do not drop your guard. Continued success, and good luck."

I was all excited and looking forward to working with detectives Egan and Grosso and other detectives from SIU, as well as other agents from my group whom I had yet met.

Fitz' message of "Big Cases, Big Problems, little cases, little problems," was a meaningful statement that I found to be relevant and applicable not only in law enforcement, but life in general.

In law enforcement illustrations of this message can be seen a little more clearly. When a case is made for instance against some unknown character, no one hears or knows anything about the case. Truth be told, no one really cares so there's not much to be concerned about.

Conversely, if you make a big case against a well known celebrity, or a distinguished politician, the notoriety is sure to bring about some form of controversy. Therefore, you better have concrete evidence to support the allegations made against the accused. Moreover, you better know what the hell you're talking about or you are sure to face serious consequences.

10

The French Connection Case

There's nothing that can be said about "The French Connection Case" that has not already been said. It was one of the greatest narcotics investigations in the history of drug enforcement. It's been talked about at local pubs near and far, and it was the subject of a bestselling novel and an Academy Award–winning movie.

If you're not familiar with the case, it was a joint effort by a team of detectives from the elite Special Investigations Unit (SIU) of the NYCPD, led by Eddie Egan and Sonny Grosso—two stellar narcotics detectives in the unit, and a group of FBN agents, led by Group Supervisor Ben Fitzgerald and his assistant, Senior Agent Frank Waters. Headquarters for SIU was in downtown Manhattan at the Old Slip Station (1st Pct.) close to the Fulton Fish Market, while FBN headquarters were also in downtown Manhattan, at 90 Church Street by the former Twin Towers buildings.

At the time, Chief Inspector Edward Carey, the Head of the City's Narcotics Bureau at (SIU) and George Gaffney, the District Supervisor of the (FBN) New York Office, had met and agreed on a mutually acceptable plan to be implemented immediately. This plan called for the Narcotics Division of SIU to assign a number of detectives to assist in the investigation led by Egan and Grosso. Similarly, the FBN, under the leadership of Group Supervisor Ben Fitzgerald, would assign a handful of agents, led by Frank Waters, to work together as teams and assist SIU in its mission.

Notwithstanding their individual reputation, the plan emphatically called for the detectives and the agents to avoid conflicts due to personal agendas, individual needs, egos and strategies. FBN would provide radiophones and other technical equipment and would also set up a 'Central Base Radio System' to facilitate the process of communications amongst all the investigators.

Since its inception (circa October 1961) through culmination (circa Jan. 1962), the case was a long, tangled expedition filled with round-the-clock surveillance, rigorous and grueling foot work, as well as hazardous pursuit driving. Despite the highs and lows, the disruptions and interruptions, it was the dogged determination of the detectives and the agents involved in the investigation that led to the culmination of this case; the arrest of Patsy Fuca, a major narcotics trafficker and the nephew of "Mob Boss" Angelo Tuminaro and his brother Anthony in New York, as well as the French suppliers, Jacques Angelvin, Jean Jehan, and Francois Barbier.

In addition, approximately 51 kilos, or 112 pounds of heroin, with an estimated street value of $32 million was seized, making it, at the time, the largest quantity of narcotics ever seized in the history of law enforcement.

There is nothing I can add to the story of the French Connection, or any aspect of the investigation, as the case is a matter of record that has already been very well documented. And inasmuch as the case is now a matter of history, I believe at this juncture it would be appropriate to shift gears and bring attention to an entirely different aspect, that being the characters who were involved and made it happen..

In every investigation there's always some interesting and unique character(s) that you either like or dislike for whatever reason. You're not interested so much in what the character did or failed to do during the course of the investigation, but there's something about this individual that draws your attention. Perhaps it is their attitude, or their behavior or merely the presence their character evokes. It is natural, particularly when working with people in high pressure situations, to be curious about the people you are working with, who they really are and what they are all about as human beings.

To that end, the aim here is to share my experience(s) and my perceptions of the guy I was assigned to work with – the sharp, rough and tough Detective Eddie Egan, featured in the movie, as that wild and crazy character we all came to know as "Popeye Doyle."

To begin with, Egan and Grosso were indeed iconic and legendary figures in the law enforcement community and their reputation preceded them. Stalwarts in their own right, they were stellar detectives who were well-known and highly respected. Undoubtedly, among the best the NYCPD had to offer.

I had met Grosso while working on a case with Waters who introduced him to me in a bar on West 96th Street and Amsterdam Avenue. Operated by a guy named "Pepe," who apparently knew them fairly well, the place was somewhat of a watering hole that served as a rendezvous for local residents as well as police officers and agents.

A sharp street guy from Manhattan, Grosso was a low key and laid-back guy who was equally as comfortable talking sports as he was about music. He enjoyed talking baseball, was an avid Yankee fan, and enjoyed discussing musical standards as played on a popular radio program at the time called "It's Make Believe Ballroom Time." Despite his reputation as a stellar detective, he was a humble and down to earth guy who always took the time to talk to you or anyone seeking advice regardless of risk.

I first met Eddie Egan one chilly afternoon at the outset of the French Connection case sometime in October 1961 at the FBN office at 90 Church Street in Manhattan. Both he and Grosso were scheduled to meet with Frank Waters that day. However, only Egan showed up as Grosso got tied up on some personal matters.

While Egan conferred with Waters, I was by my desk reviewing a case file on Jose Centeno, a fugitive from one of our pending investigations. The case had been assigned to me by Group Leader Ben Fitzgerald. Centeno was the same guy I had identified from a bunch of pictures that Waters had asked me to look through when we first met.

Every morning at the FBN office we had meetings of all agent personnel. The meetings were conducted by Fitzgerald, during which time we discussed law enforcement issues, updates on major investigations and the whereabouts of fugitives from pending cases. Some of the fugitives, like Centeno, had expressed their willingness to cooperate with the government and would stay in touch with the office. However, Centeno had been missing for some time and his whereabouts unknown. Fitz had initially given the file and picture of Centeno to Waters who then shared the materials with me.

At one of the meetings the photo of Centeno had been passed around and I recognized him as one of the "Mambo Aces," a highly successful "Two Man Professional Latin Dance Team" that performed every Wednesday at the Palladium Ball Room on West 52nd Street and Broadway. At the time the trend in Latin music in New York was at its highest peak and every Wednesday the Palladium Ballroom, (Home of Latin Dance Music in New York), hosted dance contests among the patrons during its "Amateur Night" competitions. The event also featured dance exhibitions by famous professional dancers of Latin music such as "Augie and Margo," "Cuban Pete and Millie" and the "Mambo Aces," aka "Andy and Joe." Centeno was Joe's last name and I was sure he was the fugitive we were looking for.

I was familiar with the event as I myself had participated in the competition a few years back before I became an agent. I had recognized Jose Centeno as one of the "Mambo Aces" and mentioned this to Fitz, who immediately assigned me to the case, telling me, "That's good information Louie G. Be sure to mention this to make Frank (Waters) aware and see if you guys could locate Centeno. If you do, have Waters and another agent bring him in. I don't want to expose you and who you are by making an arrest in that place. It's not a good idea to have people know who you are especially when you might have to be there on undercover assignments."

As Egan and Waters talked, I approached Waters with the Centeno file, at which time he introduced me to Egan as Louie G, the new Spanish-speaking agent. After an exchange of greetings, Egan asked me where I was from. I said Brooklyn, and he immediately replied, "That's a good beginning because I'm also from the City. Frank also tells me that you speak fluent Spanish, so tell me, how is it that you speak fluent Spanish?"

"Well," I replied, "I'm Puerto Rican born, Brooklyn bred, and both of my parents spoke Spanish which was their native language. When they came to the U.S., they settled in the Sunset Park section of Brooklyn where I grew up. My father, a military man, had taught me some English and I further developed the language growing up in Brooklyn."

"But my mother, recognizing that from that point on I'd be in school speaking English all the time, just as I would also be speaking English in the neighborhood playing with other kids, my mom insisted that I speak to her in Spanish for fear that I might forget the language.

I continued to speak to her in Spanish, but after a while I began talking to my father in English. And so I grew up speaking both languages fairly well."

Egan replied, "That's a good story, Louie G, and I believe you. But, I'll tell you what. No way are you all Puerto Rican."

"What do you mean; no way I'm Puerto Rican? Look, I'm Puerto Rican born, Brooklyn bred, and if you like, I'll show you my birth certificate. It's that simple."

To which Egan replied, "Listen, pal, you might have told these people that you're Puerto Rican and think you've got them convinced, but I'll lay heavy odds that you're not really all Puerto Rican."

And I said, "Well, in that case, what am I? What the hell do you think I am?"

And Egan stated, "Try Scandinavian."

"How the hell did you arrive at that?" I asked.

"Listen, pal, I told you before, I'm laying heavy odds that you're very much Scandinavian."

I couldn't help but break into laughter. This guy was serious. In the past I had been told that I looked Cuban, Spanish, Irish or Italian, even Greek, but never Scandinavian. I said, "What the hell makes you think I'm part Scandinavian?"

"First of all," he said, "you don't look Puerto Rican, and I have friends that are both Puerto Ricans and Scandinavians, and you look more like my Scandinavian friends. You sure don't look Puerto Rican."

I immediately told him, "Look, I hate to disappoint you, but I'm Puerto Rican and if by chance there's some Scandinavian mix in there, I think my parents would have told me. And if there's another piece to the puzzle, I don't know what it is, but if I had to guess, I'd say a Spaniard from Spain since that's the mother country. I've never explored that aspect of who I am, nor have I given it much thought. To the best of my knowledge, I'm just Puerto Rican. Sorry to disappoint you. So, let me ask you something. Why the ethnic comparisons? Isn't that just stereotyping? What do you think?"

Egan responded, "Oh, oh, you're not going to give me a lecture on all that ethnic and racial stuff, are you?"

"No, I'm not," I said, "but tell me, what does a Puerto Rican look like? What does a Scandinavian look like?"

He said, "Look, Louie G, let us not overreact or get upset, but do I look Irish to you?"

"Yes," I replied.

"Well," he answered, "that's based on appearance. No?"

"Yes," I said.

"Well, I told you, I have Scandinavian as well as Puerto Rican friends. In fact, I have three Puerto Rican friends at the station house, all of whom are great detectives. Two of them are males and the other, a female. They're all Puerto Ricans from NYC, like you, pioneer Hispanics on the job, and they look more Hispanic than you do. Now, that may be stereotyping, but it's based on appearance just as you said or agreed that I looked Irish."

I didn't mind, nor did I let the ethnic comparisons bother me as I've been taken for everything except for what I really am. It's just that I couldn't figure out why Scandinavian? I kept thinking, Mediterranean, maybe, but Scandinavian, I didn't think that was even close. But, truth be told, and in fairness to Egan, it was not the only time it had been brought to my attention.

Many years later, a lady named Pearl (now deceased) and a good friend of my wife, would sometimes ask my wife, "Are you sure Louie is Puerto Rican?"

"Why?" My wife would ask.

"Because I don't think he's P.R., I really think he's a Spaniard with a heavy mix of Scandinavian in him. Did you ever ask him?"

"No," my wife answered, "because I don't know and I don't care. It's never been a topic of discussion nor have either one of us thought about it. Should he ever find out that he's part Scandinavian or anything else, we'll talk about it." And for years that was a subject of discussion between the two whenever they visited each other or got together.

Moreover, Linda Williamson, a dear friend who worked in the State Licensing Office of the Commission at Belmont Racetrack and coordinated my retirement dinner party when I retired from the NYS Gaming Commission once asked me, if I was part Scandinavian. And I said, "No, I'm Puerto Rican."

Linda, well- known for not mincing her words, was quick to respond. "Listen Mister, she said, your last name may be Spanish, but you're part Scandinavian, and if you don't believe me, you better check your ancestry because you, Senor, are part Scandinavian."

While these comments came from three different people, all of whom were friends, two of them, Egan and Linda, did have something in common, they were both proud stubborn Irish who firmly believed that their perception was always accurate. Nevertheless, it had become an amusing but interesting issue.

Egan went on to say that whenever I happened to go to the station house (Old Slip), I'd see for myself what he was talking about. Egan then said to Waters, "Listen, Frank, since you're in charge of assigning the agents, make sure that when you see an opportunity, assign Louie to work with me. When he comes to the station house, I will show him what I mean. I also know that as a new agent, at some point, Louie will have to interact with some of the guys at SIU. Therefore, when you assign him to work with me, he'll come to the office, and I'll introduce him to some of the best detectives he'll ever work with, both Scandinavian and Puerto Rican. Is that okay, Frank?"

"No problem," Frank said, "he'll be with you next week, but first things first. Louie's got a file in his hands and it appears he wants to talk to me about something. Is that right, Louie G?"

I said, "Yes, that's right." And then brought Waters up to date on the case regarding Jose Centeno.

Waters replied, "That's fine, we'll comply with Fitz's request and we'll go to the Palladium and try to find this guy. But all in due time, okay? Right now, the focus is on this case that we're working jointly with the city. Listen, we've got Patsy Fuca and his mob connections and a few Frenchmen who are driving us nuts as we follow them by car and on foot throughout the city. We need as much help as we can get. But don't worry, we'll find the time for Jose Centeno."

"No problem," I said, "you call the shots."

Waters continued. "Look, I've got schedules and assignments for some of our guys, including you, who will be working on this case with Eddie (Egan) and Sonny (Grosso), as well as other detectives from SIU. Hopefully, we'll try to squeeze a visit or two to this Palladium Ball Room, in between assignments, or maybe one night I can switch schedules and I'll go with you."

Egan quickly said, "Can I go along when you decide to go? It sounds like a cool place to go. I'd love to see some of that mambo dancing. I love all that shit. Besides, two guys dancing, that sounds interesting. This guy [Centeno] is an entertainer, and he's paired off with another male partner. And they don't dance together like Fred and Ginger? Man, I'm not only curious but anxious to see how they pull that off. By the way, I'm going down to the office. I'll take a look at our files and see if we have anything on Centeno and I'll get back to you guys. We might be able to help you out in finding this guy. But, I'll keep you posted, okay?"

Throughout our conversation I couldn't help but notice that Egan seemed like a fun and gregarious type of guy. Although his comments seemed to have an element of sarcasm, I don't think he was serious about it. And while he seemed full of enthusiasm and ready for fun, I would not want to be on his bad side.

As we were about to part company, Egan asked me, "Hey, Louie, do you play ball?"

I assumed he was talking either baseball or softball, and I said yes. I told him that I had played baseball in high school and in sandlot ball in the PAL, Kiwanis League, in Marine Park, Park

Circle, Dyker Heights and other places in Brooklyn. I also told Egan that I played a lot of stick ball.

Egan said, "Really, were you a three sewers man?"

I quickly answered, "No, I was a two sewers man. In either sport, I was a line drive hitter, not a long ball hitter."

"I figured that. Very good pal," he said. "Were you in the military?"

"Yes I was," I replied.

"What branch?" He asked.

"U.S. Army."

"Oh, the Army, I thought so," He continued. "I was a Marine."

"Why," I inquired. "Are you the only branch that protects the country or do you ask the Army, Navy and Air Force for help when the need arises?"

"Listen, we're the toughest and the best. We don't need help."

"Really," I quipped," I thought you were just part of the Navy."

"Listen pal, I don't want to bust your bubble but the Marines are the best and they're the toughest of them all, both in war and peace. No way are the others even close."

Knowing I was talking to a Marine and this wasn't going to stop, I said to him, "Look, this may never end, so here goes. I've got two questions for you. Will you answer them for me?"

"Oh, oh, I see you're getting defensive. But go ahead, take a shot."

"Okay, here goes. Do you guys use different bullets than the rest of us? And the other question is, do you know the difference between the Army Platoon and the Marine Platoon?"

"Oh, you're also a comedian, but since you're an amateur comedian, I'll let you go first and tell me what the answer is."

"Well," I said with a wry grin, "since you don't want to answer the question, let me say that I was under the impression that we all have the same weapons, we all have and use the same bullets. Right? And as to the differences in platoons, well, regardless of the number of men in the platoon (since that may vary), you guys have one more guy than we do, and that's your publicist."

"Oh, you are getting defensive. Not to worry, next to the corps, I'll take the Army."

"That's very thoughtful of you," I said. "But I think I have a right to articulate my biases. After all my father was a World War II vet who retired from the army after twenty two years of service. I wasn't as generous with my time, but I did give them two years minus six months having served overseas."

"Wow, this is fun," Egan started, "I'm enjoying all this shit. We have a few things in common my friend and I get the feeling we're going to have some fun as we work together."

"Fine," I said.

As I left, Egan emphatically stated, "By the way, I'm still laying odds that you're Scandinavian or you have some Scandinavian in you."

I couldn't contain myself from laughing, not because the statement was hilarious, but simply because of the serious manner in which he said it. His demeanor seemed candid and unpretentious, and his genuine, but comical delivery, made it sound real funny except for one thing. He was dead serious about the issue and his beliefs. He was very forthright and seemed to be the type of person who would say exactly what was on his mind without regrets. "Sure thing," I said. "I don't know what odds you're laying, but I want part of that action."

Although it was our very first meeting we seemed to have 'hit it off' and I had learned something about the man they called "Popeye Doyle." I had also learned that he was referred to as "Bullets Egan" which would have to be the subject of another discussion. Perhaps I should have challenged him on the question of the bullets, but since we'd be working together there would be time for that later. Nonetheless, we both got along as we became acquainted and got to know each other. It had been a good beginning.

11

Surveillance with Egan

everal days later at the FBN office, Waters informed me that I was assigned to work with Egan and that I should meet him the following morning at 8:00 a.m. at the Victoria Hotel in midtown Manhattan. Waters also told me to be careful, because Egan was a very sharp detective but a slick type of guy with a propensity to exaggerate and he always wanted to be in control. I asked Waters what he meant by that and could he be more specific. He said, "Not now, but don't worry, you'll find out soon enough and you'll see for yourself."

Frankly, I was a bit unclear, but figured I'd probably find out on my own, so I agreed to do as we'd discussed and then left. From that point on until the culmination of the case, I was assigned to work with Egan many times and that comical quality would always manifest itself in his behavior, mostly in the form of quips.

The following morning, upon entering the lobby of the Victoria Hotel, I ran into Egan who was completely disheveled and looked tired and worn out. We exchanged greetings, and I said to him, "Holy shit, you look like a train wreck."

He said, "You're being kind. I feel worse than that, and I probably look it."

"Yea, but you can handle it, you're a Marine," I said.

"Okay," he replied, "you defended your team well so you can stop beating me over the head."

"I'm not beating you in any way, just having fun is all." I continued, "Let's get down to business so fill me in."

Egan then told me that Barbier, one of the Frenchmen [Frogs – French suppliers], was supposedly staying at the hotel, but the son of a bitch had not yet surfaced. Perhaps the guy left the hotel and Egan had not seen him leave. Egan had to wait for one of his colleagues to relieve him, at which time he would point out Barbier to the relief man who didn't really know who Barbier was. I said to Egan, "If you think you could hold out for another fifteen minutes, I'll go get us some coffee."

He said, "That would be great, pal. I really appreciate that."

I purchased a couple of containers of coffee with a cheese Danish and returned as quickly as I could. We ate together and lingered about the lobby area for hours.

Egan then asked me if I was upset about him saying that I looked more Scandinavian than Puerto Rican. I reassured him that I was not. As crazy as it sounded at first, I realized it may not be the last time I heard it.

He visibly relaxed. "You're cool, my man. I had a feeling about you."

"Good or bad?" I asked.

He said, "Good, of course, and besides, Frank [Waters] told me that you were the agent that made the case on Salzano, the guy who murdered Freddie Truppa. That's a good case Louie, and you're just starting out, but remember that as an undercover agent you're in a very vulnerable position. Remember that you could have also been a murder victim in the case, so be careful, my man, be careful. We have information on those guys, so if you ever need any help, let me know."

"Thanks for the advice," I said, and then I asked Egan to fill me in on their case and who was the person staying at the hotel.

Egan said, "Louie, this is a big case with the potential to be one of the biggest, but right now we're putting the pieces of the puzzle together, and we don't know exactly who's staying here, and who's staying at the Edison."

"And we're going crazy with the surveillance both on foot as well as by car, Uptown, Downtown, Brooklyn, Manhattan, Bronx. A circuitous route everywhere we go. We need a fucking compass. But don't worry, you'll soon know as much as we do."

Egan then asked me if I was still playing ball.

I said, "I stopped playing baseball after high school, and I haven't played real baseball since I became an agent."

But the agents at the office had a softball team and I'd been playing with the team and it'd been a lot of fun. Egan asked me for additional information on the team and who we played. I told him an agent by the name of Gabe Dukas managed the team, and we played other federal agencies like Secret Service, ATF, and the FBI. I informed him that the games were played at Central Park. Egan then asked me if I would talk to the manager and see if we could arrange for our team to play an exhibition game against his team. Egan, with a smirk on his face and in a sarcastic tone, said, "City kicks Fed ass…it has a nice ring to it, doesn't it? Maybe it can even become a political slogan."

I said I would speak to the manager and get back to him asap, but also warned him not to get too cocky. The headline could also be, "Feds crush City," a comment he dismissed with a sarcastic laugh.

We remained in the hotel lobby for the next several hours maintaining surveillance, but at the same time talking about everything from soup to nuts. We talked about the Salzano case, and he told me he'd heard that I had done a good job. I thanked him and then inquired as to whom we were to keep our eyes on. Egan indicated that Francois Barbier, one of the Frenchmen, was staying at the hotel. But if any of the other Frenchmen showed up, we'd also tail him. We continued to talk and get further acquainted. The conversation, I thought, was genuinely candid, and we seemed to have hit it off. Egan also told me that the surveillance of the Frenchmen, as well as Patsy Fuca, had become a rather hectic and chaotic journey. "When you're dealing with limited manpower, and you are constantly on the go to so many different locations throughout the city, surveillance becomes grueling and frustrating," Egan stated, "Some teams of agents haven't had a decent night's sleep in more than a week." I was listening and learning.

Several hours later, a man exited from the elevator, and I learned from Egan that it was Francois Barbier, one of the Frenchmen. I kept Barbier under observation as he loitered about the hotel lobby, when suddenly I was joined by Agent John Ripa from our office who said he'd been sent to replace me. Ripa and I then began looking for Egan who had suddenly disappeared from view.

Ripa said he was under the impression that SIU had a room at the hotel and Egan, who had gone so long without sleep, had probably gone to get some sleep. We then noticed Barbier about to leave the hotel. Ripa and I agreed that I should follow Barbier wherever he went and Ripa would remain at the Victoria and wait for Egan or any other detectives that might show up.

As Barbier left the hotel, I followed him on foot. Barbier walked very casual like, but periodically looked behind him to see if anyone was on his tail. I followed him cautiously to the Edison Hotel where he entered and proceeded to the house phone in the lobby. As Barbier spoke on the phone, I went for a quick trip to the men's room, and when I returned to the lobby area by the house phones, Barbier was nowhere to be seen.

I called the telephone communications center (base station) and left a message for Waters, but he was not available. I remained in the hotel lobby for about one hour and again called the base station. Waters had left a message for me to call it quits and return to the office the next day. There I divided my time working periodically with Egan while, at the same time, I continued working undercover and making buys for my colleagues at FBN.

Approximately one week later, I was again assigned by Waters to work with Egan, whom I contacted and agreed to meet the following afternoon at about 2:00 at SIU headquarters at the 1st Precinct, the Old Slip Station.

I had heard about Egan's famous quip, "Did you ever pick your feet in Poughkeepsie," but I dismissed it as a prank or just someone trying to be funny. Little did I know that I would be a witness to a similar scenario that afternoon?

As I got to his desk, Egan was interviewing a female who had obviously been arrested for drugs. Egan told me to sit down and relax as he was almost finished. I took a seat by his desk and, after asking the female a few basic questions, I clearly heard him ask the woman, "Did you ever pick your feet in Poughkeepsie?"

"What?" Asked the female.

The very serious reply was, "You heard me. Did you ever pick your feet in Poughkeepsie?"

And she said, "Man, are you crazy? I ain't never been to Poughkeepsie."

This went on a few more times, and the woman finally stated, "Listen, you know God damn well I was busted with a couple of nickel bags. So, why the bullshit about Poughkeepsie?"

Egan said, "Lady, don't get smart or things could get worse, okay. Now listen, we've got a female up in Poughkeepsie, a hooker to be exact, with a couple of felonies for drugs. She attempted to throw her pimp out the fucking window. Luckily, we got there in time. But she fits your description and so we're checking out all possibilities. We leave nothing for chance, so don't take it personally."

The female, surprised and confused by this line of questioning, said, "Yeah, but you know me, my name's Audrey, and you were there with Kelly once before when they locked me up. And besides, I'm no hooker; I just like to get high."

Egan said, "Yeah, Audrey, you're right, but you're also a very good actress, and this woman fits your description to a 'T.' How do I know you're not trying to put one over on us? Like I said, we leave no stone unturned. But, don't worry, if you've never been to Poughkeepsie, then obviously you've never picked your feet there, so you'll have nothing to worry about."

"Hey, Jimmy," he said out loud to another agent across the office, "will you take over from here? Me and Louie gotta go to midtown and replace two guys who've been on duty all night. All right? Thanks Jimmy."

As we were about to leave, the phone by his desk rang a couple of times. An impatient Egan, who appeared to be somewhat annoyed, answered the phone and said, "Harrington, Ballistics, what do you need, a couple of shells checked? What? No shooting, an assault? Domestic dispute, over drugs? Hold on, that's a different extension." Egan then hollered out, "Hey, Jimmy, there's a call for you." Egan returned to the caller and said, "Listen, Mister, if you get cut off or nobody gets on, call back and ask for Detective O'Brien, okay, he'll take care of you. Thank you, I gotta go. All right, Louie, let's go, pal."

As we walked to his car, I said, "Could I ask you a question?"

"Yeah, sure, go ahead," he said.

"I heard through the grapevine, that you've used that Poughkeepsie line before. But, since I just witnessed it in person, what the hell did that have to do with her case and what the hell was that 'Harrington, Ballistics' all about? Is that a routine of yours? It seemed to me that the call was for another person in another department and you passed it on to someone else in a very cavalier and indifferent attitude. The Lord only knows how critical or important the call might have been, and you go ahead and dump it on some other guy. Jesus, Mary, and Joseph, that was bizarre."

Egan replied, "Louie, my friend, I've been around long enough to distinguish the difference between meaningful telephone calls and bullshit calls, and to separate the bogus from the real. Besides, what sounds bizarre to some is therapy for others."

I quickly said, "Wait a minute. How can you ascertain within minutes, even seconds, the difference between bullshit, as you put it, and legitimacy, or a real call?"

Egan indignantly replied, "Listen, Louie, I like you, pal, but I don't think you've been on the job long enough to pass judgment on such situations. I'm sure that you're aware that the job we're in, we're dealing with the scum of the earth. You know how many weirdos and assholes we deal with during the course of one day? Well, let me tell you people can go crazy or have a mental break-down trying to deal with them or rationalize the nature of the call. Do you know how many people like her we arrest daily? Do you know how many phone calls, like that last one; we get during the course of the day? Well, everyone deals with the lunacy of the job differently. For me, it's a form of therapy. That's how I maintain my sanity. By being myself. But you don't have to worry about that, man, you're the feds, you deal in a different environment. You deal with more sophisticated shit. You deal with the elite; that's a whole different ballgame."

"Yeah," I said, "I guess they have a different kind of illness or a more sophisticated problem. Right?"

"That's right, buddy, you got it. You're catching on, my man."

We got into his car, a 1961 wine-colored Corvair, and Egan pulled out like he was competing in the Indy 500. "We gotta move quick, pal. We're going to replace Dick Auletta and another guy, I think Kelly, and both of whom have been on duty round the clock."

Egan continued. "By the way, when we get to the Hotel Edison, if we should come into contact with any of the Frogs, I'd like you to follow them wherever they go. If they remain at the hotel, stay on them, but as soon as you get a chance, call the base station and let me know where you are and we'll try to hook up later. All right?"

"Will do," I said.

Upon reaching the premises of the Hotel Edison, Egan dropped me off, wished me luck, and told me to stay in touch. I entered the Edison Hotel and remained in the lobby for a while.

The last time I had been at a hotel was when I was with Egan at the Victoria. One of the Frenchmen (Barbier) had left the Victoria and I had followed him here, the Edison, where he was joined by Jean Jehan, but later disappeared.

Approximately one or two hours later, I observed Jehan enter the hotel, accompanied by Barbier and another male I did not know. They lingered about the lobby, then went to the front desk at which time the third person left.

Both Jehan and Barbier then entered the elevator. I proceeded to get into the elevator with them. When the elevator reached the 6th floor, they made believe they were getting off but did not, and remained in the elevator. Upon reaching the 9th floor, both men got out, and I exited the elevator with them. With only the three of us getting off, the two men looked at me curiously and exchanged puzzled glances.

To remove any suspicion, I quickly began to talk very rapidly in Spanish. The two men looked at each other, and then looked at me again with puzzled glances, appearing somewhat confused. Whatever they were thinking, I was hoping they thought I was some kind of oddball or some jerk.

They continued to walk one way as I walked in the opposite direction. I saw them enter Room 909 which turned out to be Jehan's room. I left in the elevator, remaining in the hotel lobby for another couple of hours during which time I made a few phone calls while maintaining surveillance to determine if any of the Frenchmen left or entered the hotel.

I periodically checked with the Base Station and left messages for Egan, whom I met later on, and informed him of what had taken place. Egan said, "Good job, my man. You followed them to Room 909, which is where Jehan is staying. That's good undercover work and that little scene where you started to talk Spanish, that was cool. I wish I'd been there so I could have seen their faces. The element of surprise, I love that shit. It reminds me of when I played Santa Claus. That was fun."

I asked curiously, "Santa Claus?"

"Yeah," he shouted, "Santa Claus. Listen, Waters told me you're a good undercover agent, and I believe him. I heard about the Salzano/Truppa case, and you did a good job. But, can you play Santa Claus?"

"Maybe I can," I said. "But first, I wanna hear about Santa Claus."

Egan replied, "Well, I'll try to make it quick." He told a story about him posing as Santa Claus during which time they arrested a couple of dealers with bundles of heroin. In fact, it worked so well that he dressed like Santa a couple of times and trudged through Harlem and made a few arrests. Egan loved telling me that he'd also posed as a hot dog vendor and even a priest.

He was grinning at me when he said sarcastically, "And you probably thought I couldn't do undercover work, right?"

I said, "No, not at all, you're obviously a very clever impostor and that goes a long way toward displaying your versatility as a detective."

I mentioned to Egan that I had spoken to Dukas, our team manager, and he said that as soon as the city was ready to play ball, we'd play them. Dukas just asked that he be given a few days' notice so that he could secure a field in Central Park. "Man, that's great!" Egan said. "I'm gonna try to round up enough guys to put a team together as soon as I can."

I told him not to wait too long for fear it might start to get real cold. Egan said that despite the time constraints and the crazy scheduling, he would try and get enough guys to field a team. "Sounds great, Louie G. By the way, you did a great job today, and I'm going to mention it to Waters. Call me as soon as you're gonna work with me again. I'm sure it'll be real soon. Now, I gotta go to meet Sonny and a couple of other guys. We've been tailing Patsy Fuca from Brooklyn to the Bronx, then to Manhattan and back to his house in Brooklyn. Everything is going well, and we should be wrapping things up very soon. Take care, I'll be in touch."

12

Irish Luck – Good and Bad

I spoke to Gabe Dukas, our team manager, to determine when we could play Egan's team, and he told me that, given the nature of the investigation we were involved in, it didn't look too promising. However, he said that if Egan's team could find its way clear some evening within the next couple of weeks, we could play an exhibition game in Central Park. Dukas further suggested that we try to play the game before the real cold weather set in. If we waited too long, it would bring us into cold weather and we would then have to put the game off until spring. "But," he added, "it would be nice to squeeze one or two games in before the weather starts to change."

After speaking with Dukas, I called Egan and made him aware of the situation and he said he would try like hell to get a team ready by Thursday of the following week. Plans were quickly formulated to ensure adequate coverage for the ongoing surveillance for several hours until after the game. The following Thursday, at approximately 6:00 p.m., both teams gathered at Central Park for the game.

It was a chilly late November afternoon, and the weather had not been too cooperative, as it had rained intermittently throughout the day. Nonetheless, we played the game and we won (6-5). Despite the loss, Egan had gotten two big hits in the game, a huge double and a mammoth home run, tying the game on both occasions. After the game, I went to congratulate Egan on the home run he'd hit. It was a 'Moonshot' that traveled a long way. It was quite a blast. As I shook his hand, he grudgingly said, "Thanks, but we should have won, and by the way, you did pretty good yourself."

I had two hits myself, a double and a single. But it paled in comparison to the mammoth blast he hit for a home run. "Thanks," I said, "but we won and that's what counts."

I thought that he'd played exceptionally well. When you've played ball long enough, you can easily tell the guys who have been offered tryouts with Major League Baseball teams. It shows. I told him that he was a hell of a ballplayer and asked him if he'd ever been contacted by a major league club.

He said, "Yeah, the Yankees."

"I thought so," I said. "You showed why you got that tryout."

"Thanks," he said, "but you do realize you were lucky, you know that."

"How so?" I asked. "You're not going to blame the weather, are you? We played under the same conditions."

"No," he said, "but you guys didn't give me a chance to put our real team together. Those were a bunch of guys we got at the last minute. We couldn't get our entire team together. A couple of guys were on special assignment, a couple on sick leave. We couldn't field our 'real' team."

I said, "So, what you're telling me is, that you played with a bunch of scrubs, is that right?"

"Hey," Egan answered, "you said that, I didn't. Besides, remember that the score was tied at 5-5, and how did you get the winning run? On a cheap hit, that's how."

I replied, "It doesn't matter the type of hit, it's the score that counts."

"You're right," he said, "but come on, that hit was something I wouldn't brag about. But, that's all right; we'll get you the next time."

I replied, "Listen, pal, Irish wit may last a long time, but Irish luck does run out. Don't you think?"

"Never mind," he said, "we'll get you the next time." He kept moaning and repeating, "Luck, pure fucking luck. They beat us on a cheap miraculous hit. Luck, pure fucking luck."

One thing became clear, just as his Irish wit manifested itself in his behavior, so did being a sore loser. The guy hated to lose, something I totally identified with.

We were fortunate enough to squeeze in one game, but the next game would have to wait till spring as it was made clear to us that we would not be able to play each other again until this case was over.

During this time, surveillance of Patsy Fuca and the "Frogs" had intensified. We were working more, sleeping less, and tensions were mounting. In any investigation, you frequently lose sight of one or more of the suspects. This case was no different, as Patsy Fuca, the main suspect in the investigations, suddenly vanished. And Egan's reputation for being overzealous and his cocky attitude made it easy to jump to conclusions and blame him as the cause. But having spent time with him and observing his demeanor and the way he went about his business, I certainly did not believe it was his fault. Nonetheless, surveillance had been increased and an exhaustive search was on to find Fuca. Neither Grosso nor Waters were happy campers.

The relationship between Egan and Waters was an interesting one. They were stellar investigators but at the same time, they clashed frequently. They were both stubborn Irishmen whose competitive spirit manifested itself every time they got together. Losing sight of Fuca provided a forum for either one of them to blame the other. They always seemed to find themselves in a climate of confrontation and this was no different. In fact, if Fuca was not found soon enough, a confrontation was inevitable.

Waters, trying to be as professional as he could, hesitated to be openly critical of Egan or to blame him for losing Fuca or for anything else that might have gone awry. He was also very much aware that Egan and Grosso were not only partners, but close friends.

Grosso knew and understood Egan very well. There was no doubt as to what side Grosso was on. But, for all of Egan's flaws, Waters also had his share of flaws and that certainly could not be overlooked. Fortunately or unfortunately, we were dealing with two knowledgeable and experienced law enforcement officers who had a personal dislike for one another for reasons best known to themselves. But, it was also very clear that they were also two hot-tempered and stubborn Irishmen who were not very big on patience and usually wanted to do things their way. Truth be told, the fact of the matter was, they were cut from the same ilk.

While there was no secrecy or mystery that the two didn't get along, it was hoped that it would not interfere with the way the case was being conducted or how it might conclude, even though that was unlikely to happen given the top officials who were calling the shots at both SIU and FBN.

By this time, supervisory personnel from both agencies had met and discussed strategies for bringing the case to an end within the week, as the arrest and search warrants that had been obtained were about to expire. As for my situation, this would probably be the last time I would be working with Egan, since I was not allowed to get involved in "roundups" or making major arrests for obvious reasons. There was no point in revealing my true identity when it wasn't truly necessary. I understood that. It was not the first time that it happened, nor would it be the last.

It had been quite an experience in which I learned more about the man they called "Popeye" and how naturally entertaining he could be. I had developed a friendly and healthy relationship with

Egan, and the experience for me had been very productive and most rewarding. It had indeed been a privilege and an education combined with a lot of fun.

Surveillance of Patsy Fuca and the Frogs had been intense for the past week or so. Patsy Fuca and the Frenchmen had eluded surveillance and had been missing in action. Their disappearance had been a source of discontent with Waters who speculated that Egan was to blame for the vanishing act. However, it was Egan's contention that Patsy Fuca was still around as he'd recently spotted him in the vicinity of 45 and East End Ave. in Manhattan.

It was now the night before the warrants expired and the infiltrators would be arrested, which would bring about a culmination of this case.

There was a meeting at the FBN office concerning the execution of the search warrants; preparation and strategy regarding the arrests of all defendants; the confiscation of large amounts of drugs; and the specific locations where the defendants would be arraigned.

In the interim, there was also a heated argument between Waters and Egan that escalated into an altercation, during which time a couple of punches were exchanged between the two men. However, even the fisticuffs would not preclude the team from moving forward to carry out the plan for the arrests. Moreover, Egan's comments and his hunch that Patsy Fuca and the Frogs would be meeting in the area of East 45th Street and East End Avenue were validated. There was consensus at the meeting that Egan was right. As a result, there would be a sizable group staked out in that area, and care must be taken not to arouse suspicion and have plans go awry. In addition, surveillance of all the suspects would be loose.

While working with Egan in the past, he and I had decided that whenever we worked together, he would pick me up at Kent Ave. and Marcy Ave. by the entrance to the Gowanus Parkway, in

Brooklyn. It was a convenient location for us since we both lived in Brooklyn.

Finally, the day of reckoning had indeed arrived. On Thursday morning at approximately 8:00, I proceeded to our rendezvous point to wait for Egan. I was hoping that he was not angry enough as to preclude him from picking me up. However, I was confident that he would not let any hard feelings get in the way, and my perception about the guy was validated as he arrived about 8:30.

I got into his car with a big grin, and I asked him not to take his anger out on me if in fact he was still angry. But Egan quickly answered, "Never happen, my friend. Besides, I'm not angry. I'm probably just as frustrated as everyone else who's assigned to the case and I'm sure that everyone is hoping that it will all end today. Listen, Amigo. You have nothing to do with the fact that Waters and I don't get along, which I'm sure you're already aware of. Anyway, you have a curious grin on your face, so what's up?"

I said, "Well, my friend, that Irish luck of yours prevails again."

"What do you mean? What are you talking about?" Egan asked.

"Well, at the meeting last night, a number of issues were addressed regarding strategy, preparation for today's arrests, and the expiration of the warrants. But, more importantly I thought, was the way everyone seemed to rally around you. There was consensus that you were right as to Fuca's whereabouts and that Fuca would more than likely be meeting with the Frogs in the vicinity of 45 East End Avenue NYC." I kept watching Egan's eyes to garner his reactions, but none came. I'm sure he would have been a deadly poker player. "As a result," I continued, "a sizable group of investigators will be staked out in that area for today's expected roundup."

"Did Waters object or react to all this?"

I told Egan that Waters was in agreement with everyone else and did not challenge anyone or anything. In fact, he was rather acquiescent about everything.

Egan replied, "Great, I don't want him to get upset over all this shit."

"Great, now let's get started."

As is often the case, evasion by suspects during surveillances was nothing new, especially in big cases like this one. Some of the radio phones had become inoperable, and anxiety and frustration was prevalent. Tensions were high, and one could almost feel the knots in the stomachs of some of the investigators.

As we drove, I explained to Egan that I'd been instructed not to get involved in any roundup or major arrests such as the ones we were anticipating, lest my identity as an agent be revealed. Egan, who was aware of that, stated, "Well, that's true, and although it's a valid point, I don't necessarily buy it in this particular case."

"Why not?" I asked.

Egan replied, "Because this case is mostly about Patsy Fuca and those fucking Frogs. My feeling is that the theory might hold water with regards to Patsy because he's a scumbag and unless we flip him, he might turn out to be troublesome and rat you out in the streets if he knew who you were. But he won't know who you are, so I don't think there's a problem there. As to the Frogs, frankly, I don't think you'll ever see those fucking Frenchmen ever again. But I would generally agree, there's no point in exposing you, especially since you'll be working undercover throughout the city and the Lord knows what's going to happen to Fuca."

We drove to the Manhattan side of the Brooklyn Bridge and parked under the bridge with an excellent vantage point. We waited on word as to when Patsy Fuca left his home and in what vehicle. Since I wasn't going to be around when the suspects were rounded up, I decided to tell Egan how much I had enjoyed working with him. It had been an honor and a pleasure, and I hoped that we might work together again in the future.

Egan quickly said, "Whoa, my friend, no one is dumping anybody, and you're not getting rid of me so easy. Listen, I still have to get some information for you on that fugitive, Centeno. And remember I want to help you find the fuck. But I must tell you; my gut feeling is that the guy may be dead. I heard you tell Waters that Centeno had expressed his willingness to cooperate and has not been seen since. So listen, Amigo, I've been in this business a long time, and I'll lay the same odds or the same kind of money on you being Scandinavian that I will on this guy being dead. Okay?"

"Well," I replied with a renewed smile, "I think your chances are greater on Centeno being dead than my being Scandinavian. I have a birth certificate."

Egan replied, "We shall see. Perhaps we'll come up with a death certificate for Centeno, but the other thing is the next softball game. You are going to give us another chance at kicking your ass. Correct? Or are you getting worried because this time we'll be fielding the regulars and the outcome will be different. In other words, the next time, we just might kick your ass."

"Keep dreaming, pal," I said. "I'm looking forward to the game, indeed."

As we talked, we suddenly got a message that Fuca had left his house in Brooklyn some time ago and based on the route he'd taken, Fuca would be passing by us, so be on the lookout.

Shortly thereafter, Egan spotted Fuca in his blue Oldsmobile, driving right by us. Egan shouted, "Okay, my man, this is it!" As we pulled out, he shouted again, "The shit's on, brother!"

Once again, with Egan as wheelman and myself as navigator and radio man, we quickly moved in hot pursuit of Patsy Fuca, who was heading north on the East River Drive. I immediately notified others on surveillance that we were on Fuca.

Having noticed that Egan was driving a bit too aggressive and getting a bit close, I reminded him to give Fuca free rein. Egan said, "Thanks for reminding me." As we passed the East 42nd Street exit, I radioed that Fuca had not exited at 42nd Street but, if he was going to the East End Avenue location, he'd probably exit on East 61st Street. Sure enough, Fuca exited on E. 61st Street and drove north on York Avenue. It appeared that he was headed to the 45th East End area. Upon arrival in the vicinity of East 84th Street and East End Avenue in Manhattan, Fuca double parked his Oldsmobile and picked up three Frenchmen, one of whom was carrying a suitcase.

I radioed the information to others on surveillance, telling them that things were happening fast. Fuca soon dropped off the Frenchmen and was now headed downtown. It was slowly becoming a circuitous journey, but we were in pursuit of Fuca who we believed was now in possession of the suitcase. Meanwhile, a choppy radio call came in from Grosso, who informed us that they had a problem. A bit of chaos and confusion had set in as a result of a screw-up, and he asked us if we could join him as soon as possible. Although the radio phone was not working well, the urgency of Grosso's call came through clearly.

We were in hot pursuit of Patsy Fuca, who was headed downtown, so Egan initially declined to comply with Grosso's request. But I explained to him that the sense of urgency might very well be that they're in some kind of trouble and I thought it would be the appropriate thing to do.

Egan said, "What about Patsy, he's still got that suitcase with him? Are we just going to leave him alone? A lot can happen in a short period of time."

I told him the respite would be short, as we'd make a quick appearance and, depending on how serious the problem was, we would return to our pursuit of Patsy as soon as possible. Egan reluctantly agreed, and we turned around and headed uptown to join Grosso and the rest of the gang.

Upon meeting Grosso, we learned that pandemonium had broken loose there as they'd decided to hit the two Frenchmen who had gotten into a Buick with foreign plates. But when they hit the Frenchmen, they came up empty and they now have two French nationals they've detained for no apparent reason and they might have to suffer the consequences.

Egan hit the ceiling. "What the fuck can we do? Listen, you're in deep shit, but I'm sure you'll think of something. Louie and I were on Fuca who had picked up all the Frenchmen, one of them with a suitcase. Fuca drops them off and is headed downtown with the suitcase, and you guys up here are making a fucking mess of things. I'm leaving. Come on, Louie, let's go find Patsy."

We got back into Egan's car, and I told him that fighting with our own when they need all the support they can get, is not very productive or helpful. Egan said, "You're right, pal, but at this moment, we gotta focus on what we're going to do now and we can't be worrying about the mess created by others."

Egan stepped on the gas, and we flew out of the area and headed downtown toward Old Pike's Inn with no vehicle or suspect to follow, nothing except Egan's instincts. As we reached the area, I couldn't believe what I was seeing. Egan's Irish luck had surfaced once again, as we spotted Fuca's car by Pike's Inn. We waited for a while, and then Fuca got back in his car and headed downtown towards Brooklyn. We followed Fuca to his residence in the vicinity of 67th Street and 12th Avenue in Brooklyn.

A short time later, we tried communicating with others, but the radio phones were not working. Egan suggested that while he maintained surveillance on Fuca, I go look for a telephone booth in the area and inform all others where we were and give them an update. I complied and made my way to a public telephone booth to the calls.

When I returned to the location where he'd parked, Egan was not there. I figured Fuca had probably left the area and Egan was in pursuit. I waited in the area for about one hour, and then decided to return to the base station at FBN headquarters.

13

Success and Reflection

L ater that same day, at 90 Church, we learned that the warrants that were about to expire had been executed and a number of arrests were being made. At the same time, we also learned that approximately 11 kilos, or 24 pounds, of heroin plus an arsenal of weapons was found and seized at the home of Joe Fuca, Patsy Fuca's father, in Brooklyn.

In addition, 40 kilos, or 88 pounds, of heroin in the form of 88 single packages were also found and seized at the home of Tony Fuca, Patsy Fuca's brother, in the Bronx. In total, approximately 51 kilos, or 112 pounds, of heroin were seized with an estimated street value of $32 million, making it the largest amount of drugs ever seized by any law enforcement agency in the United States.

Legal proceedings followed and details were being sorted out as to who would be charged and who would not. Subsequently, all three members of the Fuca family, Patsy Fuca, his father Joseph, and his brother Tony, were arrested, as were the two key Frenchmen, Francois Scaglia and Jacques Angelvin. Furthermore, approximately $500,000 disappeared. Jean Jehan, who evaded prosecution because he escaped, and another Frenchman, J. Mauren, who got away, were probably the only ones who would be able to ascertain what happened to the money.

A couple of weeks later, I spoke to Egan, who called to remind me that as soon as the dust settled, I should book another soft ball game, and I said I would. Egan also informed me that one of his stools [informants] had told him that he, the informant, had learned from a friend that Jose Centeno was not dancing anymore because his partner had cut him loose due to Centeno's problem with drugs. Egan suggested that since I was familiar with the Palladium, I might consider going there with Frank, do a little undercover work, and inquire from people there that I might still know and corroborate the story.

Egan also reminded me that he wanted to tag along when we did go to the Palladium as he wanted to help us find Centeno, while at the same time; he wanted to see the pair of male dancers, the Mambo Aces, do their stuff. I agreed and told him I would notify him as soon as I found out when we were going.

After consulting with Waters on the matter, we agreed to go to the Palladium the following week on a Wednesday evening that featured the dance exhibitions by the professionals as well as the dance competition. The Palladium was located on West 53rd Street and Broadway, and we agreed to meet at a neighborhood bar on West 53rd Street and 7th Avenue about an hour before the dance exhibitions actually began, to discuss some form of strategy for the evening. We decided that I would be working undercover and hang out at the Palladium as a patron, mix with the dance crowd, and see what I could find out.

In the interim, to get more updated information, I decided to call a friend of mine, Al Angeloro, who was incredibly knowledgeable about the history of Latin music. An attorney by profession, Al was equally as well versed in Latin music as he was in law. Al had his own radio show of Latin/Jazz music, and he loved challenges. A bit of an iconoclast, he disagreed and argued with those in the Latin community who truly believed that Salsa music was an exclusive of theirs. Al was always ready to invalidate that perception and to qualify and counter-qualify his argument. To prove his point, he had traveled as far as Japan and returned with a small Japanese Salsa band that could compete with the best in Latin music.

As a true aficionado of good Latin/ music, Al would go to different countries and return with different foreign Salsa bands, thus becoming a well versed, well known, but highly controversial figure in the Latin community.

I called Al and asked him about Centeno and the "Mambo Aces." Al stated that he'd heard that they were no longer together because of Centeno's problems with drugs. Although not completely certain, Al suggested, I should go to the Palladium, hang out for a while, mix in with the dance crowd, dance with other patrons and inquire. He was confident I would quickly find out all I needed to know.. He said to let him know when I was going to be there and we'd meet and bring ourselves up to date. In the interim, he would also try to get more updated information with other sources in the music industry.

Egan and Waters, who had pictures of Centeno, would mingle at the nightclub as patrons, while at the same time, maintain surveillance and keep their eyes focused on Centeno, if he was still part of the Mambo Aces dance team.

We met as planned that Wednesday evening at about 7:00 PM and after a brief meeting, we parted company. I entered the Palladium at about 8:00 and quickly noticed that it was going to be really crowded. Furthermore, two of the biggest name orchestras in Latin music were appearing that night, Tito Puente, recognized as the king of Latin music, and one of his biggest competitors, Tito Rodriguez, was also on hand. I noticed on the billboard that "Augie and Margo" was the only "celebrity dance team" scheduled to appear that evening. The names of Cuban Pete and Millie and the Mambo Aces were not on the billboard.

I became a bit nostalgic as I lingered about. After all, I loved to dance, it was my forte. I remembered that being a good dancer made me a better ballplayer and opened a few doors for me professionally. Moreover, it's also been a tremendous tool when working undercover.

As I loitered about the nightclub, I quickly remembered that the celebrities would congregate on the left side of the ballroom as you faced the bandstand, where the professional dancers hung out. The elite amateur dancers would congregate on the right side. I got myself a drink and proceeded to infiltrate the right side where the amateurs gathered.

I watched people dancing for a while, and then did some dancing myself. I felt good as I started to warm up. It was like riding a bike, you never forget. However, I needed to infiltrate the professional side, as this is where I would probably be able to get meaningful information about Jose Centeno. Although it had been quite a few years since I had been there, not much had changed. I hung out and danced a few numbers, and then moved on to the professional side. Meanwhile, I recognized my friend Al who was talking to a group of people by the bandstand.

I approached Al, and when he saw me, we hugged and embraced. Al was a friend who knew I was in law enforcement. He also knew what I was looking for. We had a brief conversation during which time he confirmed that Centeno had been dismissed by Andy, the senior partner, who had gotten himself a new partner. Al further stated that he was inclined to believe that Centeno had been murdered when it was discovered that he was an informant.

Al asked me if I was still dancing with that redhead. And I said, "You mean Louise?"

"Yeah, that's her, you guys made a good team."

"Thank you," I said, "but we danced a few exhibitions at the Havana Madrid and the Saint George Hotel in Brooklyn under the name of Louis and Louise and that was it."

Al said, "Now that you're in a different profession, I trust you're no longer dancing."

I nodded in agreement and said to him "Unless it becomes necessary."

I asked Al to join me for a drink, and we proceeded to the bar where we resumed our conversation. As we walked towards the bar, I noticed Egan and Waters by the bar, engaged in what appeared to be a dramatic and quite demonstrative conversation.

Al went on to say that the word on the street was that Centeno was a junkie who had become a stool pigeon and had been killed while rehabbing in Lexington, Kentucky. He also stated that Andy had found himself a new dance partner to replace Centeno. While the new dance team continued giving exhibitions, they were not going to be appearing at the Palladium that particular evening.

Al and I talked for a while longer regarding a new rhythm that was being introduced into Latin music. The music, which concentrated heavily on flutes and violins, was called "Charanga," while the dance was called "Pachanga." Al, being the expert that he was, continued to talk about leading musicians with the new rhythm. I thanked Al for the information he'd provided, both in the musical arena as well as the information on Centeno. I told him that I'd be in touch, and I discreetly worked my way over towards where Egan and Waters were stationed. I told them I'd meet them at the bar where we had met earlier in the evening on West 53rd Street and 7th Avenue within the hour, and they agreed.

14

Centeno, Winning and Farewell

When we met, I told them I had obtained fairly good information on Centeno, but Egan and Waters still seemed to be engaged in an intense discussion over the dancing they had observed. Frankly, I couldn't believe what I was hearing. The two were comparing the dancing they had seen at the Palladium with the Irish jig, each using his own rationale as a basis for comparison. They turned to me and asked for my opinion between the Irish jig and the dance Angeloro referred to as "Pachanga." I explained to both that we would continue the conversation on the dance after we discussed Jose Centeno.

Neither had anything to report on Centeno other than they had confirmed through the bartender that Jose Centeno was no longer part of the group as he'd been dismissed. Waters said that he asked the bartender if he knew or had seen Centeno lately and the bartender related, as had so many others by this time, that Centeno was simply no longer with the dance team. Egan reiterated what Waters said, but added that they didn't want to press the issue of Centeno with the bartender for fear that he might become suspicious and they didn't want to take any chances. Egan stated further that he had spotted a NYC detective that he knew at the nightclub, but he didn't want to approach him for fear that the guy was working undercover. He certainly didn't want to blow the guy's cover.

Egan couldn't resist adding to his commentary, "By the way, I saw you clicking your heels, Amigo. That was cool, man. For a Scandinavian, you've got some pretty cool Latin moves. I would say you still got it. Man, this undercover work has no limits and it pays off I bet, doesn't it?"

I thanked him for the compliment and, because he was a ball player, I told him how dancing had helped me in making the pivot when making the double play at 2nd base. To which Egan replied, "I love it."

He went on to say, "I knew it, saw you play, remember? What puzzled me was, can Scandinavians dance as well as they play ball?"

We switched the conversation back to Centeno, and quickly brought each other up to date. Based on the information we'd gathered, there was no doubt that fugitive Centeno, and the Centeno from the Mambo Aces, were one and the same. It was also confirmed that Centeno, who had turned to drugs, had been let go by his senior partner. Furthermore, he'd become an informant and it was my feeling that, once word got out on the street, he wouldn't be around for long. The information we had obtained coincided with the information on the case file, and that would be sufficient to close out the case.

As to comparisons between the Pechanga and the Irish jig continued, I suggested to both Egan and Waters that we leave that conversation for the expert dance critics. There seemed to be general agreement that there were some similarities in the quickness and timing of the footwork. Besides, it was all a matter of perception, and I didn't think there was any point in trying to validate any one's perception. It was good to watch the latest on Latin dance music and then make comparisons to the Irish Jig. It made for great conversation.

We got what we went there for and enjoyed ourselves in the process. Besides, they both came away with a bit of "cultural enrichment." We all agreed, had a beer, and then went home. Egan of course had to have the last word and said, "Listen, Amigo, Frank and I don't agree on too many things, but we did talk a little about you. Both of us agreed that no matter what you call yourself, you're still part Scandinavian. In fact, the next time we get together, I'm going to bring one or two of my Scandinavian friends and take this to a higher level, okay, Louie G?"

I replied, "As you wish, my friend, as you wish."

I closed out the case, and I didn't see or hear from Egan until one or two months later when our teams played the last of the scheduled games. It would probably be the last game we played against them, because they weren't in the league and if we did play them, the games would be exhibition games, which were unofficial.

One late chilly afternoon in April 1962, we played them for the last time, and again we beat them by one run (9-8). Once again, Egan displayed his batting prowess as he got a couple of hits, including a mammoth home run.

After the game, a few players from both sides gathered together for a couple of beers. I recognized a couple of the detectives, and as we talked about the game, one of the detectives, Charlie Kelley, somewhat surprised and baffled by the results, shouted, "I don't believe this shit, man. I don't understand it."

I asked Kelley, "What is it you don't understand?"

Kelley, in angered frustration, replied, "I don't fucking believe it! We're better than these guys. We've got a couple of guys who have gotten tryouts with major league baseball teams. Anyone who knows anything about the game would acknowledge that we're the better team. But each time we played these guys, they've kicked our ass."

I answered by saying, "Wait a minute, each time we won by one run…that's not exactly kicking your ass."

"I don't care," Kelly said. "One run or ten runs, they've beaten us. I don't understand it. I can't figure this out."

Egan, who had been quiet throughout the entire conversation, quickly responded, "Oh, that's easy, I figured it out."

Kelley, still puzzled, said, "Yeah, then tell me, cause I can't figure it out. What is it you figured out?"

And Egan responded with one of his typical straight out of the 'Egan Playbook' comments. "Listen, you gotta remember, they're the Feds; we're the City. They work and deal with the top echelon of the international arena, the ambassadors, diplomats, etc. Consequently, by dealing with the elite, they get top quality stuff."

"What the fuck does that have to do with it?" An angry Kelley asked.

Egan responded, "I'll tell you what it means. They're using PURE SHIT, and we're using GARBAGE, that's why, that's the answer. It doesn't take a fucking genius to see that we have a better team. We've got bigger guys, better athletes, and more experienced ballplayers. But, again, they're using quality while we're using garbage and that leads to better performance. And I don't want to hear about team play. Every time we played them, they beat us, whether by one run or five runs, but they beat us. I'm simply saying that's the only answer. They're using pure shit and we're using garbage, okay? That's it, that's the answer, end of story, case closed."

It was a classic comment, straight from the Egan Playbook of Quips, by none other than the master, Eddie Egan himself. All present, including myself, broke out in such laughter that some of us dropped our beer cans and roared. We continued having a few laughs, and just before we parted company Egan looked towards me and said, "I love the way you dance while making the pivot at 2nd base, Amigo. Not bad for a Scandinavian."

While I never saw Egan again, I did hear of his *French Connection* exploits. Both he and Grosso became technical advisors in the movie, and while Grosso went on to become a successful producer, Egan continued to pursue an acting career in Hollywood that didn't go very well. Furthermore, he ran into some difficulty with the personnel department of the NYCPD regarding his retirement benefits. I heard through the grapevine that he was struggling financially, and although he was earning some income as a part-time actor, making cameo appearances in some movies and bit parts in others, it wasn't enough. He struggled economically, but continued to live on. I continued with my career as an agent with FBN, but I was subsequently transferred to Miami, and then to New Orleans where my career ended.

Approximately thirty-plus years later, or sometime in 1995, I heard from law enforcement friends that Egan had passed away. I felt compelled to go to the wake, and when I got there, the funeral parlor was full to capacity as I expected. Most of those in attendance were obviously law enforcement people, many of whom I recognized. I met a few of Egan's family members, one of whom was a nun, who I believe was his sister. She was a lovely lady who led me by the arm and then pointed to the coffin. I paid my respects, knelt by the coffin as is customary and said a prayer.

As I knelt looking at him lying there in peace, I couldn't refrain from saying to him, "You were right, pal. Since our discussion on the subject, there were a couple of other people who have told me that I looked Scandinavian—a lady friend at work and one of my wife's friends. But you, my friend, were the first. You were always a step ahead of the rest. You were very insightful and had great instincts. It was an honor to have worked with you, my man, although it was for too short a period of time. God Bless and Rest your soul, Amigo."

15

The Ambassadors Case
Diplomats: Pardo-Bolland, Jose Arizti, and Rene Bruchon

This investigation actually began after Mauricio Rosal, the Ambassador from Guatemala to the Netherlands, was arrested by FBN agents in New York City on October 1960 for smuggling huge quantities of narcotics into the United States. At the time of Rosal's arrest, approximately 250 pounds of heroin was seized.

Ambassador Rosal was part of an international ring that was supplying huge quantities of heroin and cocaine to members of organized crime in the northeastern part of the United States.

During the course of the investigation, it was learned that three other diplomats, Salvador Pardo-Bolland, the Mexican Ambassador to Bolivia; Juan Arizti, a member of the Uruguayan Foreign Ministry and Rene Bruchon, a French national and former Ambassador to Switzerland—also had links to the same smuggling organization.

The three diplomats were under investigation by FBN, the French police (French Surete Nationale) and the Royal Canadian Mounted Police, for allegedly receiving, concealing and selling large quantities of heroin in the United States. The drugs were being imported from Nice, France through Canada and into the United States.

On February 10, 1964, information was received from the French police indicating that the investigation had intensified. It was learned that all three men were in France and were on their way to move a large quantity of heroin from France to Canada and then onto New York.

Pardo-Bolland had registered at a hotel in Cannes, France, and the following morning, he was observed to meet with Arizti at the Cannes railroad station. Two days later, Bolland was observed to leave his hotel and drive away in a car accompanied by two men, Gilbert Coscia and Jean Baptiste Giacobetti, both Corsicans. The two men were co-conspirators in the investigation as they were alleged to be the "Corsican Connection" for the drugs. Shortly thereafter, Bolland, Coscia, and Arizti were seen together at Arizti's hotel.

On February 15, 1964, after two separate meetings between the four men, Arizti left France by plane and headed for Montreal, Canada, carrying seven pieces of luggage, four of which were given to him by a porter, minutes before he boarded the plane. Upon arrival in Montreal, Arizti, using his diplomatic status, succeeded in getting through customs without inspection.

Meanwhile, one of the RCMP had obtained legal authority and opened one of the four bags that Arizti had brought from France and found the bags to contain a white powder. After leaving the airport, Arizti went to the Montreal train station and checked the bags in public lockers. Two days later the Canadian police, again under legal authority, opened the lockers and removed the four suitcases where they found 62 kilos of heroin.

Sixty-one kilos were removed and replaced with flour, and a quarter kilo was left in each bag. The bags were then returned to the appropriate lockers. That same day, Bruchon had arrived in New York from Switzerland and registered at the Americana Hotel in midtown Manhattan. During this time, all three men had been under constant surveillance by FBN agents who had been assigned to various locations posing as taxi drivers, bellhops, and redcaps while the three men went about their business cautiously and nervously.

On February 16, 1964, Bolland arrived in New York and checked in at the Hotel Elysee, Room 1105, and at the same time made a reservation for Arizti in Room 1102 A. In the interim, the government had also occupied a room adjoining Bolland as well as Arizti's room. We "bugged" our room at the Elysee by placing electronic eavesdropping equipment on the door of our rooms so as not to trespass theirs. An electronic listening device was placed on top of the keyhole by the doorknob on the door that separated their room from ours.

We also placed a microphone on the space between the floor and the bottom of the door separating our room from theirs. This enabled us to stay within the legal boundaries and at the same time made it possible to listen to the conversation(s) taking place in Arizti's room.

On February 18, 1964, Arizti (unaware that an FBN agent was also on the same train) arrived by train at New York's Penn Station from Canada with the four suitcases containing the bags of the flour and the heroin. After checking the bags at the station, Arizti proceeded immediately to the Hotel Elysee where he checked in at Room 1102 A, the room that had been reserved for him by Pardo-Bolland. Meanwhile, another agent had secured a search warrant authorizing him to inspect the luggage. A short time later Arizti was joined in the room by Pardo-Bolland, and both men engaged in a conversation.

Since I was the only agent to speak and understand Spanish, I was assigned to listen to the conversation between the two men and translate their conversations. I had positioned myself by the door where we'd placed the electronic listening devices with a notebook and a pen. When Pardo-Bolland entered the room, they exchanged greetings and had a brief conversation concerning their trip. While I could not hear the conversation perfectly, it was audible enough for me to make notes and translate accordingly.

The men spoke slowly and clearly albeit some words and phrases were easier to understand than others. Nonetheless, I was able to get the gist of the conversation. The men were discussing the Jack Ruby trial, which was going on at the time. From the conversation, both men seemed interested in discussing the conspiracy theory, as to whether Lee Harvey Oswald acted alone or if there were others involved in the assassination. Then I overheard Bolland tell Arizti that "we will see the man that day" adding that "on business like this, one has to be very careful."

As they finished their conversation, Bolland told Arizti that he had to go to the Americana and then left the room. I quickly put my paperwork away and, along with another FBN agent, left the hotel to follow Pardo-Bolland, who went back to the Americana.

At the Americana, Pardo-Bolland briefly engaged a room clerk in conversation and then left the hotel. The other agent remained at the Americana to make further inquiry, while I left the hotel and followed Bolland, who went to the Hilton Hotel and then proceeded to the American Cable and Radio Co. where he went to an area where messages or cablegrams were sent.

Bolland returned to the Elysee where he and Arizti met again in Arizti's room and had another brief conversation. I resumed my position by the door with the electronic device and overheard Bolland tell Arizti, "I was unable to locate Mr. Blanc." They continued to talk as Bolland made mention of the crowds in the city and the energy of the people, referring to New York as a progressive metropolis. Bolland then emphatically said to Arizti, "I don't understand. In the past, the man has always been here when I arrived."

Bolland continued with his social conversation, referring to the city as a "colony of ants," and then went on to discuss various other topics. Both men seemed to be nervous and anxiety-ridden and appeared to be concerned that something was wrong or something had gone awry. Meanwhile, discussions and exchanges of information between the agents on surveillance and supervisory personnel indicated that there had been some confusion as to who Pardo-Bolland was really looking for. Perhaps, it was Bruchon and not Blanc.

The problem was rectified a day or two later when Bolland got a phone call from France. After the call, Bolland went to the Americana where he engaged the desk clerk in conversation. Bolland then proceeded to and entered the room occupied by Bruchon. Immediately after entering the room, Bolland left, returned to the Elysee and Bruchon quickly followed.

In the interim, communications and meetings between the agents and supervisory personnel indicated that all three men were getting nervous and becoming quite anxious. Cablegrams sent and received by Bolland conveyed the notion that something had indeed gone wrong. Meanwhile, due to their diplomatic status, permission had been sought and granted by then Attorney General, Robert Kennedy, for the arrest of all three men when the time came. Plans for those arrests were quickly put in place.

On the morning of February 21, 1964, the men received telephone calls telling them to leave New York immediately. Bolland and Arizti quickly went to the Pan American Airlines office and booked flights to Bolivia and Uruguay, while Bruchon went to a Swiss Air office and reserved a seat on the next flight to Switzerland. Upon leaving the office, Bruchon was observed dropping an envelope containing tickets and a set of keys into a trash can in midtown Manhattan. The keys were retrieved by agents on surveillance and used to open the four suitcases that had been checked at the parcel room at Penn Station. All three men were then arrested without incident.

At their arraignment, the diplomats all pled not guilty. Attorneys for all three made it clear that there would definitely be a trial by jury because, according to them, a substantive part of the evidence in the case was illegally obtained by the government and would not be admissible in a U.S. court.

The defense team immediately proceeded to file a motion with the court to suppress the evidence in the case. It was their contention that most, if not all, of the evidence obtained in the case was obtained through the use of electronic equipment (eavesdropping), which, under the Constitution, was illegal and therefore inadmissible in federal court. Thus, it became clear that the wiretapping issue would be their line of defense.

Subsequently, the trial commenced at the federal courthouse in lower Manhattan with Assistant United States Attorneys William Tendy and Jack Samuels representing the government and Albert Krieger and Bernard Tompkins for the defense, with the Honorable Judge John Cannella, presiding.

The trial moved steadily, as the first government witnesses testified and the cross-examination by the defense team was consistent with their belief that their clients' constitutional rights had been violated. The defense continued to argue that the evidence against the defendants had been illegally obtained by the government and was therefore inadmissible in court.

When it was my turn to testify, I took the stand and everything seemed to be going routinely. I initially testified about my surveillance of Pardo-Bolland to and from the Hotel Americana and the Elysee.

The surveillance aspect of my testimony was fairly straightforward and there was little cross-examination by the defense. Then I proceeded to testify about the report I prepared regarding conversations I overheard between the two men as they spoke while in their room.

There was no doubt that a substantial part of the case against the defendants was obtained with electronic listening devices placed in the adjoining room next to the defendant's own hotel room. Therefore, it was evident that the defense was foaming at the mouth to engage the witnesses, particularly me, in some rigorous cross-examination. Although I had been alerted that cross-examination would be rough, I did not realize that I was in for a rude awakening.

16

Cross Examination

After my direct testimony concerning the conversations I had overheard, the defense began its aggressive query on the specifics. First, they asked me if I was fluent in Spanish, and I answered yes. Then they asked me to tell the court and be more specific as to fluency. For instance, was I better in reading the language as opposed to writing it, and was I versed enough to translate and write at the same time. I replied that it was my native language, the first language I'd learned, and yes, I was fairly well versed to translate. They asked me if I was capable of translating anything and everything in Spanish, and I answered, "No, not everything."

Questioned as to what specifically I would have difficulty translating, I indicated that the translation of technical material such as engineering projects, medical terminology, or legal phraseology, would be difficult because it's very "esoteric."

Asked to explain what I meant by that, I said that most technical, medical, or legal information that is presented verbally or physically is intended to be understood by only the people in those respected areas.

Medical information or research that is disseminated to the public is understood more easily by people in the medical field. This would also apply to legal phraseology, which is understood more so by people in the legal profession. Similarly, scientific/

technical data or terms would more than likely be understood and translated by engineers and scientists.

I went on to explain that unless you had a background in the field of engineering, law, or medicine, such translations would be extremely difficult since most, if not all, of the material in those fields is particularly esoteric and understood by only those in the profession.

The defense then asked me about the report I had prepared and submitted regarding the conversations between Pardo-Bolland and Jose Arizti. Asked to explain to the court how I was able to listen to a conversation in Spanish between two men in one room and then immediately write a report in English on what I'd heard, I said that I didn't write the report immediately. The defense then sarcastically asked, "When did you write the report, a week, two, three weeks later?"

And I answered, "No, not that long. It was probably a few days later." They quickly asked me to explain how I did it.

I explained to the court that the two men spoke slowly in Spanish as they were having a casual conversation, that enabled me to write down a few key words or phrases on my notebook. They questioned how I was able to hear them. When they asked it I was in the same room I, of course, said no, I was in an adjoining room. The defense then asked me how was it that I could overhear a conversation between two people in one room while I was in an adjoining room if their room was not wiretapped. I explained that we had used electronic listening devices in the doorknob of our room to facilitate hearing the conversation. The defense then asked if it ever occurred to me that listening to a conversation by means of eavesdropping after bugging their room was illegal. I said, "Yes, I was aware of illegal wiretaps. But that was not the case. We bugged or wired our room and not theirs, which was perfectly legal."

Asked to explain what specifically the two men spoke about, I indicated that the men spoke about different subject matters, such as the Jack Ruby trial, the weather, and the crowds in New York. Questioned as to why I didn't put such conversations in my report, I replied that such information was irrelevant. The only information I wrote down was anything that I thought was relevant and applicable to the investigation. The defense then told the judge that they did not question Agent Gonzalez's knowledge of the language, but they sought to challenge his ability to listen to a conversation between men in one room in Spanish and simultaneously translate same into English. The judge asked the defense team what they proposed, and they stated that they were going to give Agent Gonzalez a test. They indicated that they would have two court interpreters available, have them read from a text, and then have Agent Gonzalez translate and write what he heard and prepare a report. The court then recessed for lunch, and everyone was asked to return at 2:00 that afternoon.

Upon my return on the stand, I noticed two other individuals by the defense table (two court interpreters), one male and one female, each holding a textbook in their hands. The defense explained to the judge that each of the interpreters had been instructed to read passages from the text. I would then translate what they'd read and write it down. The judge then asked me if I was comfortable with the procedure and, if I was, we would proceed. I said yes, and the interrogation began.

The first interpreter started reading from the text very rapidly. The passage had something to do with the "Organization of American States," an organization of South and Central American countries, including the United States that held a meeting in Washington, D.C., concerning the status of Cuba in the organization.

Since the Castro takeover, it was clear that Cuba was not in compliance with the organization's policy and guidelines. The issue of their continued membership in the OAS was questionable and had to be decided on. Clearly, the interpreters had been instructed by the defense to read at a very fast pace, in order to confuse me and throw me off track, making it difficult for me to grasp and understand what they were reading, much less translate it and then write it down.

I quickly informed the judge that the circumstances in the courtroom were entirely different from those in the hotel.

Asked to explain, I informed the judge that the interpreters were reading exceptionally fast, from a political text regarding the membership of a nation whose political status was in question, which had nothing to do with the investigation. At the hotel, I was listening to a casual conversation between two men who were having a social conversation and speaking slowly. This had enabled me to listen more carefully and then translate and make notes concerning the parts of the conversation were relevant and applicable to the investigation.

The judge agreed with me and instructed the interpreters to read slower. He also told me to continue, but to stop them whenever I thought they were going too fast and ask them to repeat what they had stated, to read more slowly, or to read at the level that was comparable to that of the hotel conversations. The interpreters continued to read very rapidly, albeit a little slower. They would alternate reading different passages, but each time they tried to increase the pace, I would tell them to slow down. They continued to read passages from the text and I continued to translate and write.

This went on for the remainder of the afternoon until the following day around noon when the judge felt there was suffi-cient information to satisfy the demands of the defense team. The judge then asked the defense team if they thought there was enough content to comply or satisfy their request. The defense agreed there was and complied with the judge's decision to have me prepare a report based on what I'd heard, translate it, and submit it to the jury.

I incorporated all the notes I'd made and prepared a summary report similar to what I'd done at the hotel during the investigation. The report, which was read and submitted to the jury as evidence, stated, in part, the following:

A meeting of the foreign ministers of Latin American countries who were members of the Organization of American States was held in Uruguay sometime in 1962. While there were several issues discussed among the member nations, the main issue at the meeting was the status of Cuba who had identified itself as a Marxist/Leninist government but, technically, was still a member of the OAS.

The goals and objectives of the member nations of the OAS were aimed at achieving peace and justice, while at the same time, maintaining the sovereignty, territorial integrity and their independence and security. It was an organization founded on lofty objectives and high ideals.

Cuba's position was not only inconsistent but truly incompatible with the goals and objectives on the Inter-American Council of the OAS. The United States sought to influence the OAS members, especially from Central America, to take a hard line against the Cuban positions and actions. However, there were major differences between some of the member nations within South and Central America, some of whom were opposed to the sanctions being encouraged by the United States.

Argentina, for instance, had proposed a compromise that would have Cuba expelled from the OAS. The proposal would be supported by economic sanctions and the establishment of a national security committee.

This report was submitted to the jury for their assessment and evaluation. The jurors seemed to be well satisfied with the report and the translation as they deliberated and shortly thereafter found all three men guilty as charged on all counts of illegally importing and distributing drugs into the United States and of conspiring to violate the federal narcotic laws (receiving, concealing, and selling of narcotics). The jury rendered a guilty verdict for all three men who were sentenced as follows:

Salvador Pardo-Bolland—The Mexican Ambassador to Bolivia and The Netherlands was sentenced to eighteen years' prison to run concurrently on each count of conspiracy.

Rene Bruchon—A French national, and formerly the Ambassador to Switzerland, was sentenced to fifteen years in prison to run concurrent with each count of conspiracy.

Jose Arizti—A member of the Foreign Ministry in Montevideo, Uruguay, received a ten year sentence, also to run concurrently on each count of conspiracy.

Both Pardo-Bolland and Rene Bruchon appealed their case(s) to the U.S. Court of Appeals, Second Circuit, but their appeal was denied and their sentences upheld. All of this transpired beginning December 4, 1964 and was decided June 29, 1965 (243 Docket No. 29218).

Subsequent to the Ambassadors Case, I received an award for noteworthy contribution in the investigation. It was my second citation after receiving the first one in 1962 for *The French Connection Case*.

As the recipient of two awards in four years, it was a good feeling for a young agent on the rise. I had assimilated very well and had become fairly popular. It had been quite an achievement and I was indeed very proud of what I had accomplished thus far. However, I was in for a big surprise, as things were about to change, and not for the better.

17

Evaluation Paradox

Following the Ambassadors case, Group Leader Ben Fitzgerald (Gp.1), my supervisor, was assigned to supervise the Courthouse Squad at the Assistant U.S. Attorney's Office in Manhattan. The squad was made up of a group of FBN agents, assigned to assist the AUSA's Office, in the preparation of cases brought to trial.

Fitzgerald had been replaced by Lenny Schrier, who became the group leader. There was no secrecy or mystery that Schrier and Frank Selvaggi, another senior agent, were among the best, if not the best agents in the office. They had been the most productive and the most successful agents for some time. They were both well respected, held in high esteem, and both were well qualified to be group leaders. Both were next in line for promotion to group leader and my guess was that Schrier got the job for reasons best known to himself.

I was not too concerned about working with Schrier, as I had worked with him in the past and we got along very well. On several occasions he had asked me to make "buys" for him, and we succeeded in making a few cases together. We were both sports enthusiasts and loved talking sports. Schrier was a huge basketball fan after having played college basketball at St. John's University. We had gone to a couple of college basketball games together at the Garden, and we had become friends. But Schrier was very rigid, had a dogmatic leadership style, and was a rather harsh critic. Highly opinionated, he felt there was absolutely no reason why an agent could not make a case. According to him, anyone can make a case.

As part of his duties and responsibilities, one of Schrier's first official acts as group leader was to evaluate his agents by giving them a rating of Excellent, Satisfactory, or Unsatisfactory.

I was not concerned at all by the evaluation, as my track record spoke for itself. However, I was in for the surprise of my life when I discovered (much to my chagrin) that I had received an unsatisfactory rating. I was in a state of shock and very disturbed by the evaluation. My mind raced, full of questions; An unsatisfactory? On what grounds? What's the criteria for the evaluation?

I approached Schrier and questioned him on the evaluation, asking him if this was a joke or a mistake. "Neither one," he said. When I pointed out the number of cases I had initiated during the month, Schrier responded by asking me, "How many of those cases were for our group?"

I said honestly, "None."

"Well," he said, "you've answered your own question."

I said, "Wait a minute, that's not my fault. No agent from our group has asked me to do any undercover work for them or has asked me to help them in any kind of way."

And Schrier's response was that team players reach out to each other, they don't always have to be asked.

"What the hell is that supposed to mean?" I said. "I think you're being quite unreasonable and inflexible and not very objective, which is unlike you. I can't believe you're doing this. You've asked me to work with you many times and we've made some good cases together. What's happened? Why are you doing this?"

"Look," Schrier said, "I made up my mind, and the grade stays. Okay?"

"No, it's not okay!" I said. "Why don't you do a little bit of introspection and reassess your thinking on this. It's just not fair."

"Listen," he stated, "it's final, and this conversation is over. Understand?"

I asked him to compare my performance for the month to anyone in our group or any other group for that matter and then consider or reassess the evaluation. Schrier responded, "I don't have time to review anyone's ratings, nor do I need to compare other agents' ratings. Look, you've answered your own questions. That's it."

I continued to challenge and hollered, "Wait a minute…the idea that I didn't make a case for our group…that's not right, that's not fair. What's that got to do with it?"

And Schrier's response was, "It has everything to do with it. You work for me, and your contribution to my group was unsatisfactory. Therefore, I gave you an unsatisfactory."

"Wait a minute," I said, "I didn't know that cases I made had to be exclusively for you or for this group."

"They don't," Schrier replied. "But how many of the cases you made were for this group?"

"None," I said again, "but there was not one agent here that asked me to make buys for them, that's certainly not my fault. Furthermore, why didn't you direct them to sit down with me and with their informants and see if we could make some cases together? Perhaps you're not doing a very good job managing. Perhaps it's you who should get the unsatisfactory from your supervisor."

It was apparent that Schrier had become annoyed by the remark. Consequently, in a harsh tone of voice, he replied, "Listen, smart ass, don't make things worse for yourself. I don't want to add insubordination to the evaluation. And in addition, you've also fallen behind in your paperwork."

Because that was a valid point, I couldn't argue, but as to

the overall evaluation, I said to him, "Listen, your criteria for giving me an unsatisfactory seems to me to have been based on a cursory examination of whatever reports you might have. And it appears that whatever it is you used to evaluate, you read it with your myopic point of view, and I think it's not only grossly unfair, it's asinine."

And Schrier replied, "You're pushing your luck, Louie. Be careful with what you say."

"Why?" I asked. "What are you going to do, add an 'F' to the unsatisfactory?"

Schrier's response was, "That's it, get out, go and follow up with whatever it is you want to do."

"I assume that you're not going to reconsider?" I asked.

"No," he said, "the grade stays."

"Well," I said, "that leaves me no choice but to go over your head. I'm going to see the District Supervisor."

To which Schrier stated, "You can go see whoever the hell you want and do as you wish, but my decision is final."

There was no one to turn to but my former group leader, my friend and mentor, Ben Fitzgerald. As a group leader, Fitz also reported to Belk and that would facilitate the process of getting to Belk, who appeared to be a fair and decent human being. I really didn't know him, nor did I have any kind of relationship with the man, but Ben Fitzgerald did.

As a group leader himself, Fitz reported to Belk. When I went to see Fitz, I explained to him what had happened and his immediate response was, "At the risk of being redundant and repetitious, I told you so, Louie G. You Hispanics are almost as stubborn as the Irish. Now I don't want to jump the gun or be judgmental, but I'm willing to bet that you didn't listen to me or maybe you did. What do you think, am I wrong, Louie G?"

"You're not entirely correct, but close enough," I said.

Fitz then stated, "I've known Schrier a long time, and I have the highest respect for him. But he's off base on this one. Come on, let's go see Belk."

We went to see Belk, and after explaining the situation, Belk said, "I tend to agree with you both, but what do you want me to do?"

Fitz said, "Have the grade changed, that's all."

Belk then said, "That's going to be difficult because I'd be undermining one of my group leader's authority as well as his confidence." Belk then asked Fitz, "How would you like it if I were to undermine your authority?"

"That may be true," Fitz said. "But it also assumes that no wrong was committed here. And this is not right, and it's not just. It's simply deplorable. Moreover, when he was challenged by Louie, he was quite perfunctory. The absence of the human element is quite disturbing to me, George, and it should also bother you because it's non-existent."

Belk replied, "That's fine and dandy from a philosophical standpoint, but that's not what I need. I need something solid, relative to policy, rules, regulations, etc. So think of something more concrete than a philosophical speech."

Going into his professorial role, Fitz quickly said, "Okay, try this. Merit, not ego, should guide and dictate an evaluation. First of all, Louie G was hired by the government to assist FBN in its mission to combat drug trafficking and drug-related crimes, and thus far, he's exceeded all expectations. Louie G was NOT hired to enhance Schrier's image or satisfy his needs, any more than he was hired to enhance the group's image. Furthermore, in his evaluation, Schrier is holding Louie to a different standard than other agents in his group. There's obviously an imbalance here that must be redressed. Everyone must be held to the same standard. I'm sorry, but this is totally unacceptable. As such I believe Schrier's off base on this one."

There was a brief pause and then Fitz continued, "When you

speak to him, George, you might also want to point out to Schrier that after being appointed group leader, he never even sat down with Louie and explained to him what he [Schrier] expected from his agents."

"In this particular case, for example, Schrier could have informed Louie that although he was making a lot of cases for other groups, he was expected to spend time in his own group and figure out with other agents how they can work together and make cases for their own group. He didn't do that. You might want to remind Schrier that perhaps he might have crossed the line as he himself appeared to be a contributory factor to the problem."

Ben Fitzgerald was proving his eloquence again. "Look," he stated calmly, "this could have been avoided if Schrier, after becoming group leader, had taken the time to sit down with Louie and have a rational discourse on what he expected of Louie. Schrier could have made it clear to Louie what were his expectations of Louie and his division of labor. Was Louie going to spend all of his time working for other groups, and how much time did Louie expect to spend with his own group?"

Fitz went on. "Listen, Louie worked for me for a few years after becoming an agent. He made a great many cases, but very few for our group. I wish he could have made more cases for our group, but he was being utilized and over-utilized by agents from other groups, which has become a big problem that isn't purely Louie's fault. There are limitations. So let's be clear, I say again, Schrier's off base on this one."

Belk stated that according to Schrier, Louie had also fallen behind in his paperwork. And Fitz answered, "Oh, that one's easy, just remind Schrier that as a condition of changing the grade, there'll an asterisk by Louie G's name. The asterisk shall clearly indicate that Agent Gonzalez is not authorized to make or initiate cases until he catches up on his paperwork. Now go do your thing, George."

Belk proceeded to meet with Schrier, and after a lengthy meeting, returned and informed me that he was more confused than when he went to see Schrier. This entire evaluation process is a paradox. Belk stated that he couldn't believe what was going on. Belk said that Schrier acknowledged that Louie was a very good agent and he's delighted that Louie's in his group because he likes him very much. He's used Louie before on undercover assignments, and they made several cases together. All Belk could gather about the unsatisfactory rating was that it might be Lenny's way of forcing Louie to spend more time making cases for his own group. Briefly put, it's Schrier's version of tough love.

I immediately responded, "Jesus, Mary, and Joseph, I'd hate to see what kind of grade he would have given me if he did not like me. What about the grade?" I asked.

Belk stated that Schrier had reluctantly agreed to change the grade to "Satisfactory," but he was not thrilled with the idea. It's Schrier's notion of implementing his authority through tough love. He knew all about Louie and likes him very much, but he felt that Louie had to be reminded that it's not necessary for him to work so much for the other groups and spend a little bit more time with his own group.

Belk, talking directly to me, strongly suggested that devoting some time to my own group was not a bad idea. He understood that working undercover and making cases was not an exclusive need of Schrier's. But by the same token, I should also consider trying to make a case within my department. Besides, Schrier stated that while he may have rushed to judgment, he made it clear he was going to change the grade by the next evaluation period with an explanation. Belk told Schrier that if he liked Louie that much and he was really pleased with having Louie in his group, he should consider being consistent in his reporting of Louie's evaluation.

Belk went on to say that he told Schrier that we could solve this problem through acknowledgement that there may have been a reaction and an overreaction to an issue that certainly could have been handled differently. Belk stated that Schrier had indicated that Louie was a gutsy kid, but when he came in with a cocky attitude and some of his sarcastic comments, Schrier probably overreacted and became angered.

As to the notion that Schrier was being overruled, Belk clearly stated that there was nothing of the sort. Belk indicated that he'd assured Schrier that not under any circumstances was he undermining Schrier's confidence and authority. Belk said that he viewed the situation as one where he, as district supervisor, and Schrier as his group leader, had to find some conflict resolution to a problem that had surfaced unexpectedly.

Belk also made it clear to me that Schrier was not an ogre. Belk stated that he was very pleased with the results and he did not anticipate any further problems. "Schrier was just trying to get you more involved in your own group, but he obviously had a peculiar way of showing it."

"Well," I said, "Like I said, I would not want to know the results of the evaluation if the man didn't like me."

And Belk added, "The man is a competitive individual who, as a group leader, wants what's best for his group." Belk suggested that, henceforth, I should be a little more patient or objective and try to understand Schrier's point of view instead of calling it "myopic."

"I was upset and frustrated," I said. "It won't happen again. I will try to put some effort into working with the guys in my group and see how we can work together and make some cases for the group."

Belk quickly responded, "That's what I want to hear and I'm certain that's what Schrier also wants to hear. Now, let's make it happen."

Afterwards, I returned to the group and the atmosphere was a little bit tense, but I figured it wouldn't be long before we returned to normalcy. I also noticed that the relationship with Schrier had not deteriorated as I thought it might. In fact, he looked at me and grinned with a superficial grin as if nothing had happened. We spoke briefly and agreed not to hold any grudge towards each other. I told him that from that point on, I would try to better collaborate with my colleagues in the initiation and development of cases for our group. Schrier was delighted to hear that. We hugged and embraced and continued with the business at hand.

18

The Albert Pereida Investigation

Shortly after the incident with Schrier, I wanted very much to make a case for our group.

It would go a long way in establishing group cohesion and camaraderie. Most of the informants I had worked with were under the supervision of other agents. Inasmuch as I had none of my own, I would probably have to make the case without the benefit of an informant, which would make it very interesting and quite challenging. It would more than likely increase my workload, which meant more paperwork, but at the same time, it would also reflect a good faith effort on my part and go a long way toward strengthening the relationship with Schrier.

There were a number of bars and clubs I had patronized during previous undercover assignments. Given the atmosphere, the ambiance, I felt rather strongly that I could make a case by process of infiltration. Hanging out in the place, socializing, dancing, and being part of the dance crowd was something that came easy to me. Dancing and playing ball was my forte. If I did that, even for a brief period of time, I felt confident enough that I could make a case by buying cocaine or heroin from a local drug dealer. Hopefully, it would be a well-known drug dealer.

I had been to the Playboy Bar on East 149th Street and Morris Avenue on numerous occasions, and, since I was a good dancer, it wouldn't take me too long to mix in rapidly with the crowd.

It certainly would facilitate my meeting someone like Albert Pereida. He was a well-known drug dealer from the Bronx who frequented the Playboy Bar. Pereida, who was often seen at the place, had a reputation as a "Sharp Cat" who was well connected.

I'd learned that Pereida was the man to see if you wanted good quality snow (cocaine) or dynamite (weed). Supposedly, the marijuana was as good as Panamanian Red or Chicago Green, both premium marijuana that were often talked about on the streets, but difficult to get. Therefore, I was convinced that without the benefit of an informant, the Playboy Bar was the place to start.

The Playboy was a local bar that catered to community residents and at the same time attracted people from outside the area who wanted to enjoy themselves dancing and having fun.

The place had a big following because it offered great Latin dance music, and when you weren't dancing, you listened to the likes of Sinatra, Bennett, Ella Fitzgerald, and all of the greats. It was a popular place that served as a rendezvous for some of the local politicians and because of its music and dancing attracted a lot of people from outside the area. Besides feeling comfortable in the place and becoming part of the dance crowd, I had also met two guys named "Paco" and "Willie," both of whom were friendly with Pereida and could facilitate the process of my meeting the guy.

I made Schrier aware of my plan, and he was ecstatic, saying it was a great idea. But he wanted to make certain that I had someone covering me every time I went to the place. Schrier made it clear that under no circumstances did he want me spending time in the place without proper surveillance. He asked me if I had asked anyone in the group for assistance, and I said that although I had not been assigned to anyone team, I had thought of asking Joe Casale and Jim Ceburre, who had recently joined the group. "Good choice," Schrier said. "Tell them I said it's okay, and let's get started. Just keep me posted, you hear me," and I said I would.

Most of the agents throughout the office had nicknames, and we were no different. I had been christened Louie G by Ben Fitzgerald. Joe Casale's nickname was "Joe Cash," and Jim Ceburre was "Seabreeze." No one really knows how these nicknames evolved, but if you didn't know any better it seemed like these guys had no last names.

As individuals, both Casale and Ceburre were good friends of mine and they were characters unto themselves. Casale (Joe Cash) was born on East 116th Street in the Italian section of Harlem but grew up in Harrison, Westchester County, New York. A graduate from the College of Holy Cross, Casale was a former captain in the Marine Corps who served in Okinawa and had earned black belts in Judo and Karate. A bright guy with a clear combination of "brains and brawn," he was a tough Marine with a heart of gold. In essence, he was your "All-American" boy. But like most of us, he was not without flaws. Bold and brazen, he had a penchant for stretching the rules. And more often than not, he'd have to be reminded that he was no longer in the Marine Corps.

Ceburre was born and raised on East 138th Street and St. Ann's Avenue in the South Bronx and boasted about being a "cool" Irish/Italian who grew up amongst Blacks and Puerto Ricans by the Fort Apache section of the Bronx. He was an "All-City" football player at Monroe High School in the Bronx, and a former Navy veteran. He also played some football at the University of Miami in Florida, where he majored in finance. Ceburre and I also played on the FBN softball team. He played 1st base, and I played 2nd base and occasionally shifted to 3rd.

Casale and Ceburre had a few things in common. Both had a bit of "Runyonesque- vitality" in them, as they both reminded you of a couple of Damon Runyon characters. And both were quite "Epicurean," as both loved fine food and great wine, not to mention a great time. Each had his own credo, to be used whenever they thought it was appropriate.

Casale, a blind loyalist, held steadfast to the notion that "Loyalty denies Objectivity." Ceburre, a would-be Wall Street tycoon, loved an audience, particularly at social functions or parties, where he could espouse or reiterate his famous quote of "I'll buy and sell every one of you fucking guys."

Both were aggressive and outspoken and, together, they were quite a duo. But their biggest attribute was, they were both - stand up guys - the type of guys you want in your foxhole or whenever you're in dangerous situations. Moreover, we were all members of the same fraternity (Band of Brothers) that's been in existence in law enforcement and the military since its inception.

I met with Casale and Ceburre and brought them up to date on my plan. I informed them that it was the kind of situation where, once I met Pereida, a purchase of an ounce of cocaine could take place immediately. On the other hand, it could drag out since he didn't know who I was. There was also the possibility that all of our efforts could meet with negative results. Nonetheless, I would make every attempt to keep them posted by leaving messages at the base station.

They were elated and couldn't wait to get started. Ceburre went on to say that he was aware of the place because it was near his old neighborhood and it was the type of place where he and Joe could go in, have a drink and maintain surveillance without raising suspicion as to who they really were. They both told me they had confidence in me and knew I could pull it off. Close friends that we were, we hugged and embraced.

I told them that the following Friday evening I was going to the Playboy and attempt to purchase an ounce of cocaine if possible. Therefore, they should be prepared, as I was going to aggressively pursue efforts to make a buy from Pereida, or if not him, one of his associates.

The following Friday evening, we met and held a brief meeting to map out our strategy. We then parted company, and I proceeded to enter the bar. Perhaps it was going to be our lucky day because as I walked in, I observed Willie, one of the guys I had become friendly with, having a drink with a guy I thought was Pereida.

After ordering a drink for myself, I sent them both a drink, at which time Willie asked me to join them. Upon doing so, Willie thanked me for the drink and then introduced me to the guy who referred to himself as Albert Pereida. We chatted for a while, and when he recognized a young lady who had entered the bar, Willie excused himself and proceeded to join the lady.

At this time, I noticed both Joe Cash and Seabreeze enter the premises and have a drink by the bar. Meanwhile, Pereida thanked me for the drink and we continued talking. Pereida said, "I've seen you dance. You're a very good dancer for a guy who's not Spanish." I thanked him for the compliment but told him that in fact I was Spanish. "Where from?" He asked. "Spain, Cuba?"

"Neither one," I said. "Puerto Rican and raised in Brooklyn. Where are you from?"

"Wow," he said, "man, you sure don't look Rican. Me, I'm a Rican from the Bronx," he said. "But I can't dance like that. Where did you learn to dance like that?"

"It's a long story. I had a girlfriend who was a dance instructor and she showed me a lot. We used to dance as a team but no more, that's over."

Pereida nodded, as he seemed to understand the story too well himself.

"Listen," I said. "You're a sharp cat and you're a very popular guy around here. Maybe you can help me out."

"What's the problem?" Pereida asked.

"Look, I've got a few people in Brooklyn that I supply with snow…you know, "perico" [cocaine slang in Spanish]…and they've been complaining that it's bad shit. My connection was a good one at the beginning, but I confronted him recently and he keeps giving me excuses, telling me there's a panic out there and good stuff is hard to come by, but I don't believe it. Anyway, I lost all confidence in the guy, and I'm looking for a new connection who can give me better quality stuff."

Pereida very abruptly cut the conversation short and quickly stated, "Why did you come to me? Who told you to come and see me?"

I said, "Look, if you think someone here told me to see you, forget it. No one did. We just met. But you know as well as I do, in every business, there's a grapevine, and eventually you find out who the competition is, who's your friend, who's your enemy, and where to look. But, you can rest assured that no one here told me to go to you."

Pereida quickly stated, "Well, look, I don't know what you heard, or who told you about me, but let me tell you, whatever you heard is fucking bullshit; I'm not into that shit. Okay? Listen, you seem like a nice guy, and it's my turn to buy a drink, but let me tell you something, I'm really not into drugs, you understand?"

"No problem, my man, forget that I asked."

We had another drink, during which time I said, "Thanks for the drink, but let me say that I wasn't suggesting that you were dealing. I came to you because I've come here enough to see that you're a sharp guy who's very popular, the women flock to you and the people here speak highly of you. Therefore, I thought you'd be able to help by putting me in the right direction or referring me to someone. And the offer still holds, if you know of someone that might be able to help me, okay?"

"And by the way," I said as I rose to move on, "I'm perfectly willing to pay the right price, even more than what I was paying before. And if the stuff is of good quality, I'll come back for more. Lots more, all right? Now, let's forget what we talked about and have another drink. On me, this time."

Pereida agreed, and we enjoyed another round. I danced a little bit more, and then left the premises.

After leaving the Playboy, I called the base station and left a message for both Casale and Ceburre to meet me at the same location where we'd met prior to entering the bar. I waited almost forty-five minutes before they joined me. I asked them why they took so long, thinking perhaps there might have been some problem since that was the first time they'd been to the Playboy. Casale pointed out that everyone was dancing and having so much fun, he felt compelled to join in, so he asked a young lady to dance a couple of times. When he went to get Ceburre, he was engaged in what appeared to be heavy conversation with an old high school buddy who bought them both drinks, so he returned to the dance floor.

Ceburre quickly pointed out that he was getting set to leave when this Puerto Rican guy sends him a drink. When he went to thank the guy, the guy told him that he'd recognized him from their high school football team. Ceburre easily remembered the guy as they were both from the same neighborhood and both had been teammates on the football team as well. In fact, it turns out the guy used to hold the ball for the kicker on the football team and he remembered Ceburre as an "All-City" running back from Monroe High School.

Ceburre obviously returned the drink and both continued to talk about the old days in high school. Ceburre went on to say that every time he turned around to look for Joe, he was stuffing his face with "empanadas."

Casale took umbrage to Joe's comments and retorted, "Jim is correct in that he did run into an old high school teammate. And inasmuch as they appeared to be involved in what I perceived to be some meaningless dialogue, I decided to return to the bar and continue to have fun. And," he quipped with great emphasis, "for the purposes of clarification, I was eating "pasteles" and not "empanadas." In our agency, this is referred to as "Cultural Enrichment"; something my friend seems to lack."

At this juncture I decided to intervene as I anticipated a satiric war of words with a cultural theme. I quickly interjected, "Well, you guys seemed to have enjoyed the evening combining work and pleasure and that's fine. But did you see who I spoke to?" They both acknowledged that they saw me talking to a sharp Puerto Rican male they thought might be Pereida. They had no picture of Pereida, but remembered my description of the guy.

Because this was their first look at the guy and they didn't know what was going down, they left the bar to call base and see if there were any messages from me. They also couldn't help talking and raving about some delicious Caribbean delicacies they feasted on. It was unclear whether someone in the kitchen had prepared them or some patron had brought them in. Nonetheless, the delicacies were delicious, and Casale went as far as comparing them to some Cantonese dish he had at Jilly's in Manhattan.

Casale was adamant in delivering his succinct message. "Those fucking delicacies were great. They reminded me of Jilly's Cantonese. Damn, I haven't been to Jilly's in quite a while, so, as soon as we finish this case, we're going to Jilly's. My treat, okay? In fact, we don't have to wait till the case is over. We can go next week."

"Absolutely, we'll go," I said, "but let's finish what we started. Okay?"

Ceburre laughed and said, "By the way, that's a great idea. Let's do it. I haven't been to Jilly's in some time myself, and I love the place." I agreed to the idea, but informed them that I had not been as fortunate nor did I have as much fun as they seemed to have had.

While I had succeeded in meeting Pereida, he unfortunately didn't take the bait. In fact, when I approached him on the subject of drugs and I was looking for a new source, he was quick to point out that he was not into drugs. He denied being involved with drugs in any way, shape, or form. In fact, he became somewhat indignant. Ceburre replied, "Nothing new baby, don't they all say that."

Realizing that I would not be able to score from him that night, I told my colleagues that I had asked Pereida if he knew or heard of anyone who could help me out. I told him that because I loved to dance, I'd definitely be there next Friday. If he was going to be there, we could have another drink. Both Ceburre and Casale agreed that I had handled the situation as well as could be expected.

Despite Pereida's negative response, I told my partners that I was very confident that sooner or later, he would come through. So, the plan was to return to the Playboy Bar the following Friday, if not every succeeding Friday, until we achieved our aim of making a buy from Pereida.

19

Infiltration and Initiation

We returned to the Playboy that following Friday and the plan was the same, except this time Casale and Ceburre knew who Pereida was, having gotten a good look at him the previous week. I entered the Playboy about 9:00 PM and a short time later, Casale and Ceburre came in. They walked towards the end of the bar where they positioned themselves at a section of the bar where they had a good vantage point of the entire bar and ordered a drink.

Approximately forty-five minutes later, Pereida entered the bar, accompanied by a very attractive lady and another couple. They seemed to be in a joyous, partying mood as they exchanged greetings with several patrons, including myself. I danced a couple of times and then noticed that the other couple had separated themselves from Pereida. I sent Pereida and his lady friend a drink. When his lady friend went to talk to a couple of other women in the bar, Pereida came over and thanked me for the drinks.

After an exchange of greetings, Pereida told me that he personally could not help me, but he knew of someone who might. I said, "That's great. If the person is here, why don't you introduce me to him? I'll buy him a drink, and we'll talk business."

Pereida quickly stated that the guy was not there, nor was he interested in meeting me. Pereida stated, "My friend will deal with me because we know and trust each other."

"That's fine," I said, "but I would prefer to meet with the guy because I want to know who I'm doing business with. Suppose the stuff is of poor quality or it's bad shit, who do I talk to about that? Who do I complain to, you? Can I hold you accountable if that happens?"

Pereida said, "Don't worry about that. You're gonna have to trust me. As I told you, I'm not into drugs, but as a business man, I will never turn down the opportunity of making some bread. But don't worry, I won't allow anything bad to happen; you're in good hands brother. Besides, the guy is a friend of mine and he's a very sharp cat."

"Listen," I said, "if the stuff turns out to be quality shit, I'll be back for weight (greater quantity)."

"Well," Pereida said, "I'll let him know that. Now, what are you looking for?"

I quickly replied, "Well, I'm looking to cop some snow [buy some cocaine]. I would normally cop a few pieces [buy a few ounces], but since this is a first time with this guy and I don't know what kind of stuff he has, I'll try a piece [ounce] as a sample."

"As I told you, if the shit's good, I'll come back for a few more pieces. If the stuff is really dynamite, then we're talking weight, my man. I'm talking an eighth of a kilo or maybe a quarter kilo. Now, I don't know if your man can handle that kind of weight, but you're telling me he's a sharp cat. Well, let's see how sharp he is."

Pereida looked about and appeared thoughtful for only a moment.

"What about price?" I asked. "How much bread [money] are we talking about?"

"Well," Pereida said, "for a piece, its $600."

"Whoa," I said. "I normally pay between $400 to $500 for an ounce. Can you do a little better than that?"

Pereida said, "Not when you're talking about quality stuff. You keep talking about quality shit, my man. Well, you gotta pay for good stuff, you ought to know that."

I remembered that all I had drawn out was six hundred dollars, but I didn't want to leave myself strapped, so I said, "Well, look, you caught me completely off guard. I have the six hundred, but I need some spending money, so what if I give you five hundred and when I come back the next time, you can add the hundred I owe you to the price of the ounce. Is that okay with you? In fact, if I see you before then, I'll give you the hundred. Okay? It's just that if I give you the full six hundred, I'll leave myself broke, and I can't do that. All right?"

"Fine," Pereida said, "but don't give me the money here in public. Let's go outside."

"Wait a minute," I said. "Why don't you go get the stuff and come back, and then I'll give you the money."

"No way!" Pereida said. "Listen, man, I'm trying to do you a favor, understand? First of all, you wanna cop some good shit, but you don't have all the bread. Now you don't want to front the bread? You drive a hard bargain, my man. But, look, it's very simple, if you don't give me the money out front, you can forget it, there's no deal. Okay? And remember, I don't like doing business in public, so if you want the shit, we're gonna go outside where you can give me the money, not in the bar. Ok? I'll go get the stuff, and I'll be back in an hour. Understand?"

"All right," I said. "I'll give you the money, but when we get outside, let's go by your car because I couldn't get a parking space and my car is a few blocks away."

We left the Playboy and walked about one block from the bar and stopped by a Lincoln Continental. I asked him if the car was his, and Pereida replied that it belonged to a friend. I counted out $500 of Official Advance Funds (OAF) and gave it to Pereida who said, "Look my man, I'll be back in about one hour. So, go back to the bar and dance your ass off. The ladies will love it."

As soon as he left, I went to the nearest telephone booth, called the base station, and left a message for Casale and Ceburre that Pereida had left in a Lincoln Continental to get the stuff. I returned to the bar and noticed that Casale and Ceburre were no longer there. My guess was that they had gotten my message and were hot on Pereida's trail.

Approximately an hour and a half later, Pereida returned. Upon entering the bar, he beckoned me to go outside and join him. We walked about a couple of blocks, and then stopped by a parked car. Although not a Lincoln, I couldn't recognize the make of the car. We got into the vehicle at which time Pereida handed me a brown paper bag. I opened the bag and found a glassine (transparent plastic) envelope containing a crystal-white powder. Pereida said, "My friend swears it's excellent shit. Why don't you try it and see for yourself?"

I said, "No, not a chance. I don't want to hang around carrying shit with me. I want to leave the area quickly. Why take chances? And I've got people to see." Pereida then asked me if I wanted to join him for a drink, and I quickly told him no, but thank you.

As I was leaving, I told Pereida that if the stuff was as good as he and his friend claimed it was, I'd be back next Friday. I quickly asked Pereida if there was a number where I could contact him, and he said, "We can always meet at the Playboy. That's good enough for the time being." We parted company, and after communicating with the base station, I proceeded to meet with Casale and Ceburre at a location previously agreed to.

They indicated that they had observed me getting into the Lincoln with Pereida and, after I exited from the vehicle, they followed Pereida in his vehicle to two locations in the Bronx. First he went to Manny's Bar/Restaurant on Westchester Ave. and Elder Ave. where Pereida went in, spoke to a couple of guys, and remained for about twenty minutes.

After leaving Manny's, Pereida drove to the "Tropicoro," a popular Latin music dance club on Southern Boulevard. Upon reaching the club, the agents encountered heavy police activity in the area. Police officers were directing traffic as drivers were being instructed to go in different directions. Consequently, they lost sight of Pereida and, after circling the area a couple of times, they called the base station and proceeded to meet me at our designated meeting place.

We discussed what had taken place and then called it an evening. Ceburre secured the evidence and the following Monday the evidence was initialed, adequately prepared and safely secured. In accordance with chain of custody policy, the evidence was sent to the U.S. Chemist's Office for testing/analysis and safekeeping.

Test results indicated that the cocaine was of excellent quality. Consensus of opinion was that Pereida must have a fairly good connection (source). Since we expected to go back for the second buy, we decided to follow the same scenario.

20

Arrest and Conviction

The following Friday, at approximately 8:30 p.m., I returned to the Playboy Bar and exchanged greetings with some of the patrons I was familiar with. I sat by the bar, and a short time later, I noticed that Casale and Ceburre had entered the premises and sat themselves at a table not too far from where I was sitting.

About a half hour later, Pereida arrived, accompanied by a female and another couple. They went directly to join another couple they seemed to know and proceeded to have drinks at their table. Shortly thereafter, Pereida came over and joined me. We exchanged greetings and he said, "I didn't expect to see you so soon, but then again, you love to dance, so it's no surprise."

I responded, "Well, you're right, but remember I said if the stuff was good, I'd be back for more, so here I am. Besides, I owe you some money, and I like to pay my debts."

Pereida said, "I'm not worried about the money, and I told you that if it was necessary I'd add the hundred dollars to the price of whatever you bought. By the way," Pereida stated, "were you looking to cop something tonight? I mean, I didn't think you'd be back so soon."

I said, "Look, the stuff was so good that I was able to get rid of it quickly and make some money. I told you that if the stuff was that good, I'd be back for some weight and I will, trust me. But I made good money on the last piece and I'd like to buy another one. If this one turns out to be the same, then we're talking weight, brother. And besides, I'll need some time to get the money together."

"Listen," Pereida replied, "to buy weight will require some time because my friend also is going to need some time. Okay?"

"Yeah, fine," I said, "so will you get me a piece for tonight for the same price?"

"Look," he said, "I got you some good stuff for a reasonable price, correct? I ought to charge you more. Come on, now, don't spoil things. One hand washes the other."

"You're right, you gave me good shit for a cool price, and I appreciate that. That's why I came back so quickly. That's what makes for a good business relationship. And listen, since you gave me a break last time, I want to pay you back, so you can add the money to the price of this one and that makes us even. All right?"

Pereida said, "That won't be necessary. You kept your word, so it's on the house. The price will be $500."

"That's cool, brother, but just one favor?" I asked.

"What's that?" He said.

I said, "I'd like to take care of this as soon as we can, because I don't want to hang around carrying shit, it's too risky. Okay?"

"Don't worry," Pereida stated, "I got a heavy night tonight, and I have this chick and some people waiting on me. We're going to a dinner party, so I'm limited in time."

"So, why don't I give you the money now? Okay?"

"No," he said, "it's not okay. Not here. Give me about twenty minutes, and we'll meet outside of the bar like last time. Okay?"

"Fine," I said, as Pereida left to rejoin his friends.

Approximately twenty minutes later, I left the Playboy to wait outside for him.

About fifteen minutes later, I was joined by Pereida who motioned for me to walk with him. I thought we were headed for the Lincoln like last time, but he stopped in front of a Buick and by a street pole where the pole's light was shining on us. I counted out five hundred of OAF and gave it to Pereida. He said, "I'll meet you right here in an hour. All right?"

I said, "Okay, see you then." We parted company, and I went to the nearest telephone booth and called the base station to notify my surveillance team. I walked back to the bar, had a drink, and noticed that Casale and Ceburre were not there. They were probably on Pereida's tail.

Approximately one hour later, I returned to the area where I had given Pereida the money, but he wasn't there. I called the base station to see if there were any messages from the surveillance team. There was a message from Ceburre that Pereida had been delayed at Manny's Bar on Westchester Avenue talking to some guys and he was still there. Casale was in Manny's bar as he'd followed him to the place and Ceburre was conducting surveillance on the bar from his vehicle, right outside of the bar.

Finally, about forty-five minutes later, Pereida arrived and asked me to walk with him.

We walked about one block, during which time he apologized for taking so long, but he got tied up on some personal matters. As Pereida handed me a brown paper bag, he said, "You're not going to be disappointed my man, you're getting the same stuff you got last time. Okay?"

"Cool, that's great, man."

"Now, I gotta go, because I'm running very late, man. I told you before, I got this chick and this other couple waiting for me. We're supposed to be going to a dinner party, and we're super late."

I quickly said to him, "Listen, this is why I wanted a number to contact you so we don't have to stress ourselves out like tonight that you were late cause you were delayed and now you're under all this pressure. So, will you give me a number where I can reach you?"

Pereida said, "There's no rush on that. Come to the Playboy. I'm always there. If you really need to see me, ask Paco or Willie. They'll know where to reach me. I gotta go. Good luck, take care."

We parted company, and I proceeded to meet with Casale and Ceburre at our usual spot.

Both said that this time they saw me giving Pereida the money, and then followed him to the same two locations he'd gone to during the first buy, the Tropicoro and Manny's Bar. When Pereida got to Manny's, he ran into a couple of people he knew and that delayed the process. By this time Casale, who had followed Pereida into Manny' s Bar, saw Pereida talking to two guys.

Shortly thereafter they vanished momentarily for about fifteen minutes and then reappeared.

Pereida had a drink with the two guys and they engaged in conversation. Apparently, Pereida realized that he was running late and quickly said good-bye to a few people at the bar and left carrying a package.

Casale rejoined Ceburre and drove back to meet me at our designated meeting place. We met and had a brief conversation during which time we discussed what had gone down and where and who Pereida might have met, to determine who his source of supply.

Ceburre retained custody of the evidence until we met at the office. At that time, the evidence was processed, adequately prepared, secured, and sent to the U.S. Chemist's Office for testing/analysis and safekeeping until the trial.

The issue regarding the quality of drugs is, in my opinion, over-rated and very subjective. Whenever drugs are purchased or seized, it goes to the U. S. Chemist's Office for testing and analysis. When the office reports its findings, it's reported in terms of percentages that are generally in the range of five to ninety-five percent.

As in any other business, there's a difference between buying from the manufacturer versus a retailer or even the distributor. As with drugs, if you buy from some inferior dope peddler in the streets, the quality of the drug will usually be considerably less than if you bought it from a big-time drug dealer who's selling in kilo quantities.

As to the percentages, there is some similarity to the grading system in some of our schools where sixty-five to seventy percent (65-70%) is passing or fair; eighty to ninety percent (80-90%) is good and ninety to one-hundred percent (90-100%) is excellent. Anything less than sixty-five (65%) is not good.

When the chemist advised that the stuff was the same top quality as the first buy, the thinking was that Pereida must have a very good connection, therefore it was important that we get to his source, as he might be a big time dealer who could potentially lead us to a large seizure.

Under normal circumstances, you'd consider developing the case to its fullest potential.

However, we were restricted from working on the case further due to some pertinent information that was uncovered. A background check of records and files disclosed that one of the two men Pereida met and conferred with at Manny's Bar, was a well-known drug dealer by the name of Mike Montserrat. While he could have been the source for Pereida, Montserrat was the subject of an on-going investigation by another group. Further involvement with an on-going investigation, could bring about a scenario we were not prepared to accept. So, to avoid conflict we decided to arrest Pereida.

Subsequently arrested, Pereida did not plead guilty as he chose to go to trial. He got lucky during the first trial, as the AUSA, who tried the case, made a mistake in his summation by saying something that by legal definition was prejudicial. The defense objected to the comment, and then moved for a mistrial that was granted by the court.

In such instances, the judge could dismiss the case and set the defendant free or he could remand the defendant and have him tried again. It was a good-news / bad-news situation for Pereida. The good news was the mistrial. The bad news was that he was remanded by the judge, which meant that he would be incarcerated until he was tried again.

Within one month, Pereida was tried again, but this time he was found guilty as charged.

As best recalled, he was sentenced to either five or seven years in prison.

We were all delighted with the outcome. However, I made it clear to Schrier that despite the hard work that went into making the case, it was an investigation that was initiated and developed without the benefit of an informant. These types of cases are not easy, and that was something I would not consider doing on a regular basis.

To which Schrier replied, "I don't know about that, it's my understanding there was a lot of fun to be had, a few drinks, fine delicacies and good Latin music to dance to. And the most important thing was, another dealer was removed from the streets of New York City. Not bad, Louie G., not bad at all." I went on to tell Schrier that he must learn to dismiss such exaggerations.

In any event, the mention of delicacies reminded me of Casale's fervent desire to go to Jilly's as soon as possible. I left Schrier's company and quickly rushed to see Joe and refresh his memory.

21

Meeting Sinatra

Following the Pereida investigation, I got an early morning phone call from Joe Casale, indicating that I should make myself available on Thursday evening of that week, as we were going to Jilly's. Consistent with his remarks during the Pereida investigation, Joe, with his military training and authoritative style, made it clear that it was time to go to Jilly's, and both he and Ceburre were going and would like me to join them. He emphasized that to decline was not an option. It didn't take much convincing as I was delighted to go. Joe said that if we didn't get a chance to talk again, we would meet in front of Jilly's at 8:00 PM, on Thursday of that week and I agreed.

Meanwhile, Pete Wilkocki, another agent and friend, had come by to see me and asked if I could help him with a couple of translations. Pete stated that it was not a translation of literary work or official documents that needed to be translated. He merely wanted me to serve as a translator for two individuals he intended to interview who spoke very little English.

Pete said that he and his partner were assigned to locate a fugitive by the name of Ricardo Ramos, alias "Field Jacket," a suspect in a big case of theirs. At the time of his arrest, Ramos had agreed to cooperate, but then he vanished and had not been seen until he was recently spotted by the two individuals he was going to interview.

Ramos, a former official with the Batista regime in Cuba, had been arrested by NYCPD detectives in Manhattan in a car with a friend, delivering a couple of kilos of cocaine. The case against Ramos was rather weak, but under questioning he'd agreed to cooperate with the government. However, as often happens in these types of cases, he disappeared.

Ramos had been seen by a cleaning woman in the area at a bodega in the vicinity of West 77th Street and Columbus Avenue in upper Manhattan. He was also spotted by a waiter named Miguel having dinner with a female companion at Victor's Restaurant on West 79th Street and Columbus Avenue. Pete felt that both the cleaning woman and the waiter could provide them with key information as to the whereabouts of Ramos, but neither one of them spoke much English. They were hoping to interview both of them on Thursday, and therefore asked me if I could be available.

I agreed to help them out but informed Pete about going to Jilly's on Thursday evening with Casale and Ceburre, in the event we ran into time constraints with the interviews. Pete quickly stated that I should not be concerned. There would be no conflict. We would be interviewing both of them Thursday early afternoon thus allowing us sufficient time.

Moreover, upon hearing we were going to Jilly's, Pete immediately said that he would like to go and asked if he could join us. An avid Jazz fan, Pete had been to Jilly's on several occasions to listen to different Jazz groups and he loved the place. In fact, he'd been to Jilly's a couple of times with Ceburre, and they both enjoyed the place very much. I said to Pete it would be great to have him join us and I would pass the information on to Joe and Jimmy. I reminded him that we'd be meeting at 8:00 PM in front of Jilly's on Thursday.

Accordingly, the interviews with the waiter and cleaning lady went well as we got good information as to where Ramos was staying. Now that they had a location for Ramos, it would enable Pete and Eddie to develop a strategy as to how and when they could apprehend Ramos.

Later that evening, at about 8:30, the four of us, (Joe Casale, Jim Ceburre, Pete, and I) met in front of Jilly's as planned. A great cocktail lounge in mid-town Manhattan, Jilly's was a "Swinging Spot" for music lovers with great jazz sounds and delightful food with different types of delicacies.

Upon entering the premises, we sat at the bar, near the entrance. There wasn't much of a crowd, but it was still early. The bartender, who seemed to recognize Pete, came over, and we ordered a drink. Not too far away from where we sat, also at the bar, was a patron who seemed to be half on his seat and half on the floor. A burly, middle-aged guy, the man was leaning forward over his drink and his head kept coming forward, nodding. It became apparent that the nodding was not from drowsiness but drunkenness.

The bartender warned Pete that the guy was intoxicated and he had stopped serving him. The bartender repeated that the guy had been drinking for a while, and obviously had one too many. He'd given the man some coffee, but it didn't seem to help. When he told the patron that he was cutting him off, the man became somewhat angered, launched into a tirade and began to get loud and boisterous.

The bartender had also tried to reason with the patron, but the guy continued with his rantings, becoming excessively rude and vulgar. Frustrated and annoyed, the bartender was starting to feel extremely uncomfortable because Jilly Rizzo, the owner, was sitting in the back room with his very close friend Frank Sinatra and two lady friends.

Upon hearing that Sinatra was there, Joe, who was a huge Sinatra fan, asked the bartender, "Did I hear you say Sinatra's here?"

And the bartender replied, "You heard right pal, Sinatra, the one and only."

"Where is he?" Joe asked.

The bartender said "He's in the private room in the rear with Jilly."

Meanwhile, the patron, in his drunken stupor, continued running his mouth with vulgarities, calling for a drink and getting louder and much more obnoxious. It was obvious that some of the patrons were getting restless and annoyed.

By this time, the bartender, who'd had enough, decided to call the Police. Immediately Joe Casale said to him, "Hold on, let's give it one more try, let me go talk to the guy." Joe left our company and proceeded to walk towards the drunken patron.

As he got to the man, it appeared that Joe said something to him while at the same time Joe put his arms around him as if he was hugging or embracing the patron. We thought they were having a conversation when suddenly, in the blink of an eye, the patron looked like he was unconscious. Joe began walking towards the entrance with the unconscious patron's left hand around his shoulder.

The three of us had rushed over to see if we could help somehow. As we approached him, Joe said to us, "Can you get me a cab? This gentleman asked me to help him get a cab and he wants to go home." The patron was falling towards Joe as his left hand flew over Joe's right shoulder.

Meanwhile, the bartender was on the phone frantically trying to reach the police. Suddenly, Joe called out to the bartender, saying, "That won't be necessary. Our friend here is going home, aren't you, pal?"

We didn't know what happened. It was all so quick and so sudden. All we heard was Joe say, "Get me a cab please, this gentleman wants to go home." Because we were in midtown Manhattan, access to taxicabs was not a problem. We went outside, hailed a cab and helped put the patron in the back seat. Joe spoke to the cab driver very briefly, and we returned to the bar.

By this time, Jilly, a concerned owner, was by the bar talking to the bartender who seemed to be somewhat anxiety-ridden, but very relieved of what had taken place. Jilly couldn't thank us enough and told the bartender to give us a drink. We told him we didn't do anything, that it was all Joe. We merely helped him put the patron in the cab, after he'd apparently convinced the guy to go home.

Jilly left our company and rejoined Sinatra and the ladies. The bartender also couldn't thank us enough, but the big question remained. What did Joe say or do to convince the patron to leave? Everyone was curious and wanted to know. But no one knew.

As friends of Joe, the three of us were aware that Joe had a black belt in both Judo and Karate. Thus, speculation began that maybe it was one of those advanced and quick martial arts moves that did the trick. But if he had executed one of those, we never saw it. Furthermore, what did he say to the patron that made the guy so acquiescent to leave after being so irascible throughout the evening? Perhaps it was something Joe said, something intimidating or threatening. Whatever it was, we didn't see it, nor did we hear it. It was best known to Joe. And because he wouldn't say, it remained a mystery. Nevertheless, tension by the bar had subsided and normalcy was restored.

We had ordered some Cantonese dishes that Joe and Jimmy had longed for, and a very good Jazz quartet started to play some very good jazz sounds. Shortly thereafter, we were notified by a waiter that Jilly and his friends wanted us to join them. We really did not want to go back there, as we were enjoying the music as well as the Cantonese dishes. In addition, we didn't want to seem rude and pompous. But, the opportunity to meet Sinatra doesn't come by that often, so we decided to join the group with the understanding that we would not disclose who we worked for, or that we were agents.

If it became necessary due to unusual circumstances, we agreed that we could probably get away with saying we were teammates from a local college baseball team, like St. John's University, and we were out celebrating Pete's birthday. So, we left the bar area and proceeded to join the group sitting in the rear.

Upon joining the group, Jilly introduced Joe to Sinatra, and then to the ladies. Joe, in turn, introduced us all to Sinatra and the ladies. After an exchange of greetings, a brief conversation ensued concerning the incident with the patron, as Joe was asked what happened and how did he manage to remove the guy. They all acknowledged that it was a bold and courageous move, not to mention the risk involved. The guy could have erupted like a volcano, and the situation could have gotten out of hand. However, we were all curious to hear what Joe's response would be.

Joe said, "Let's dismiss or forget all the fuss about the incident. First of all, I went over and exchanged greetings with the guy as if we were old friends, and I hugged him. Because of his condition, as I embraced him, I immediately put a choke hold on him. Now, as you may or may not know, we all have a carotid artery by the side of our neck that provides the blood that flows to the brain. Any kind of pressure that is placed on the artery will make the person immediately unconscious, so with the choke hold, I put some pressure on the artery and out he went, at least momentarily. It is a simple procedure that I learned during my training in martial arts. The use of force wasn't necessary, and given his condition, he'll probably never know what happened. The way he was headed, he was going to be arrested and would have to spend the night in jail. He'd need bail money and what about his family, think of them. This would be a real embarrassment, and this could all be avoided if he went home right away. Of course I had him in a choke hold where a person can hardly move or speak. All you could really do is follow orders or deal with the consequences."

"How is it you didn't have to use any force?" was the question being asked among those present.

"It wasn't necessary," was Joe's response. "I was prepared for it, but it wasn't necessary, thank God, The guy grasped the situation very quickly and must have realized that the consequences were not a choice. Gotta give the guy a lot of credit, it was a wise move."

Joe was honest and candid in his explanation, but that was his nature. As friends who knew him, we believed him regardless of what others thought. His explanation was good enough for us. Nothing more needed to be said, case closed.

We had a couple of more "treats" and inquired of Sinatra if he was going to sing, and if he was, would he comply with a couple of requests we had. And Sinatra said, "You gotta forgive me, guys, but I have to apologize. My throat's a little sore from allergies. I just came back from Vegas, and I was with a couple of my friends, like Dino and Sammy. You heard of those guys, right? And I'm sorry, but never mind that, I'm interested in the requests you guys had in mind. So, if you don't have any objections, I'd like to hear."

Jimmy clearly stated, "All of Me." Pete then followed with, "Where or When," and I said "Although I have several favorites, I would have liked to hear "I've Got You Under My Skin" or "I Get a Kick Out of You." In explaining to Sinatra the reason for my choice, I indicated that I recently had a conversation with a friend, regarding great American Jazz Singers." Names like June Christy, Chris Connor and the great Ella Fitzgerald, were obviously mentioned, as were male jazz singers such as Joe Williams and Mel Torme. But when I mentioned Frank Sinatra, my friend indicated that while Sinatra was undoubtedly one of the all time greats, he wasn't sure if Sinatra could be classified as a jazz singer. I strongly urged him to listen to "I've Got You Under my Skin," found in "Songs for Swinging Lovers" and that would clarify the issue.

If that didn't answer the question, then listen to the album, "Sinatra at the Sands" with the Count Basie Orchestra, featuring arrangements by Quincy Jones and that would certainly convince him. Subsequently, I saw my friend again and he acknowledged that both albums were awesome and he absolutely agreed with my perception of the man as a great jazz singer was entirely accurate.

Ergo, my request for either of those two numbers.

At this time, Sinatra broke in and said, "That's quite a story young fella and I want to thank you for your comments. Normally I leave those type of issues to be determined by the public. And let me just say that you guys really know your music. All those songs you requested are standards from the great American Song Book, which by the way are most often sung by Jazz Singers. And, I'm really sorry fellas. I do apologize for not complying with your requests but I'm really not up to par and I hope you forgive me."

We re-assured Sinatra that no apologies were necessary, but I did mention to him that he might want to re-assess his comments about our musical expertise as that might be a bit of exaggeration.

"I don't think so." Sinatra said. "You guys are pretty sharp and you're from New York which gives you an edge. Is there anyone here from Jersey?"

"No Sir," we responded.

"I didn't think so," Sinatra said. "And by the way, you can dispense with the Sir, I haven't been knighted, not yet anyway. Listen guys, I really want to thank you guys for what you did and for taking the time. I've had a blast and I hope we can do this again. It was great meeting all of you."

At this time, we thanked Sinatra, Jilly and the ladies for their hospitality and for allowing us to share in a very pleasant and enjoyable evening but it was time to go. Jilly who had not said much throughout the evening because he'd been very busy, couldn't thank us enough. However, we made it clear to him that

Joe was the one to thank as he took care of the problem. We had not done much except support him and look after him. We have his back just as he has ours and that's a given.

As were leaving, it was obvious that Joe was totally immersed in conversation with Sinatra and was not leaving with us. He remained with the group and after saying good-bye to everyone, we told Joe we'd see him in the morning.

The following morning we talked to Joe, and we all agreed what a great time was had and how gracious and generous both Jilly and Sinatra were. We also agreed that both individuals were the complete antithesis of what the press tells you or will have you believe about these two celebrities. But, as law enforcement officers, we understand a little about public perception, especially as it's cited or reflected by the press.

However, more importantly, and much to our surprise, we learned that Sinatra made some overtures to Joe to have him join his entourage as an advisor and bodyguard. At first, we laughed it off, but when Joe said he was considering it, the three of us reacted. We were concerned, and told Joe how we felt. Obviously, it probably wasn't what Joe wanted to hear.

Each of us made it clear to Joe that it was a nice gesture on Sinatra's part and it was very flattering, but as far as we were concerned, it was a non-issue. Perhaps the atmosphere or the whole environment changed after we left, or maybe the incident that took place was misinterpreted, but it appeared that by evening's end, the whole conversation took a different turn.

Nonetheless, we made it clear to Joe that as far as we were concerned; the matter was not even open for discussion. The consensus among the three of us was that this entire matter was beyond the realm of possibility. "Are you guys saying that I shouldn't even consider it?" Joe asked.

"That's right," was the answer.

"Why? That's not fair," Joe said.

I said, "We're not talking about what's fair or unfair. For God's sake, life's not fair."

Jimmy asked, "What makes you think you're going to be one of his advisors, perhaps one of his bodyguards?"

Pete quickly interjected, saying, "Right now it's a fantasy trip, but come on Joe, you know better than that." Furthermore, he pointed out, "Did it ever occur to you that it might sound great that you're one of Sinatra's staff members, but in essence what you really are is one of his flunkies?"

"And," Jimmy added, "maybe you had one too many and you thought you were in fantasy land. But, listen, we had a great time and to some extent, it was a bit of fantasy for all of us because after all, it was Sinatra, brother."

"Listen," I said, "as a singer/entertainer, he's second to none. He's the best. I'm sorry we didn't get to hear him sing last night, but he wasn't up to it. And we understand and appreciate that. But this is a whole different scenario. You're talking about leaving a career to hook up with Sinatra and his entourage. Come on, brother, you're too smart for that."

"Look," Jimmy added, "we don't travel in the same circle as those guys. They're in a different world. They lead unpredictable lives."

"Listen," Pete added, "we had a great time and Sinatra liked you, Jilly liked you, they all liked you. You were a big hit, man. And now, you've brought this to our attention and that's great, we respect you for that. But you know how we, as friends, honestly feel about the entire situation. So, when you want to talk or further discuss the matter, reach out for any one of us. You know we'll be there."

"Well," Joe said, "thank you for your unsolicited advice. I respect your opinion, and I will take it under advisement, but the decision is mine, so I'll keep you posted as to what I'm going to do. I love you all and I'll be in touch."

By the end of the year, both Joe and Jimmy had left FBN for new and different careers in private industry. Jimmy left to join a manufacturing firm of women's casual footwear, where he became its Executive Officer. Unable to re-enlist in the Marines, Joe went to work for a prestigious insurance firm where he went on to become one of the company's productive and leading managers.

As time went by, rumor had it that Joe did work for Sinatra as a bodyguard for a short period of time. Because he was a close friend and also my son's godfather, I probably had more contact with him than the others. I also knew that he idolized Sinatra, but I was just as curious and concerned about that whole idea and sought to find out if he'd pursued the idea of becoming part of Sinatra's entourage.

We stayed in touch and would occasionally get together, so eventually I asked him if there was any truth to the rumors that he was or had been one of Sinatra's bodyguards. Joe acknowledged actually joining Sinatra's team for a brief period of time. I asked him how long did it last, and he said for a few months. He went on to say that while he appreciated the concerns that his friends shared over the Sinatra situation, it was something he did because he had to find out for himself. However, the realization that this was not the career for him came rather quickly, and he parted with Sinatra on good terms.

Joe made it clear that he had a great deal of respect for Sinatra, who treated him royally while he was there. But he was also quite candid in stating that he may have been "star struck" and, as a result, got caught up with all the hype. An outspoken individual, Joe stated that he had an honest conversation with Sinatra as to what he really wanted to do and Sinatra was very understanding about the whole situation, making the departure a lot smoother.

Subsequently, he joined one of the leading companies in the insurance industry where he went on to become a highly successful executive. We all went our separate ways. Pete Wilkocki and I remained on the job, but by Christmas of 1966 I was on my way to Miami.

22

Transfer to Miami

(Shakedown)

By November of 1966 everything was going smoothly with my life as an agent. I was the recipient of two awards for noteworthy contributions in two separate cases and was on my way to becoming one of the premier undercover agents in the New York Office. I was still a Journeyman Grade (GS-11) and was under consideration for GS-12. I was, in short, enjoying an excellent reputation that promised an even brighter future.

During the Christmas holidays of 1966, I suddenly received notice from headquarters that I had been transferred to the FBN Miami office. I didn't know what to think.

Was this a joke, or was it a mistake? Was this a common occurrence? Why me? By this time, I had a new supervisor and group leader named Ted Heisig, who had recently been transferred to New York himself. I had not yet established any kind of relationship with him, so I didn't want to ask him about the transfer. Therefore, I reached out to the person I would normally consult with, Ben Fitzgerald.

I asked Fitz if he was aware of the transfer or if he'd heard anything about it, and he said he had no idea. It was also news to him, but he would try to find out what happened.

I was somewhat disappointed by the transfer, but that was obviously a very subjective view.

After all, I had started in New York, made many friends, gained a lot of experience, and had enjoyed a very good reputation. However, when looking at the issue objectively, there was validity to the transfer. New York wasn't the only place without Spanish-speaking agents.

The Miami office was suffering from the same problem that New York and other offices in the East were having. There was a dearth of Spanish speaking agents throughout the country, but more so in the cities and large urban centers such as New York and Miami. Therefore, if you spoke the language fluently, you were in demand.

Although the Miami office was much smaller than the New York office, with only five agents, the City of Miami was being inundated with Cubans who fled the country after the revolution and the establishment of a Communist regime. Miami's Hispanic population was growing by leaps and bounds, so the transfer, from the government's standpoint, made sense. A New Yorker all my life, I was obviously not a happy camper with the move, but like a good soldier, I followed orders. So I picked up my family and during the Christmas holidays 1966–1967, we headed south to Miami.

Once in Miami, I was making my share of cases and did not experience any problems. However, there was one rather unusual incident that occurred shortly after my arrival that was totally unexpected and inexplicable, leaving me completely shocked and confused. I don't recall who specifically made the suggestion, but it had been proposed at the office that I meet with an informant by the name of M. Stern, or Marty, for the explicit purpose of making some good cases against some major violators that Marty supposedly knew well.

According to the information I was given Marty was a sharp guy who was originally from NYC, but had been a resident of Miami Beach for a long time. He was a pretentious hotshot, a wannabe mobster, who was more talk than action and had a pompous way about him, accompanied by a nasty and sarcastic tongue. He'd been reluctant to bring some agents to any of his so-called friends because, in his opinion, they lacked the undercover experience to act and behave the way his friends did. I thought it was a lame excuse, but since I didn't know the guy that was a bit unfair. Reluctantly, I decided to go along with the plan.

Rumor also had it that Marty was well connected. A former gambler, Marty supposedly had links to gamblers as well as drug dealers on the Strip and maybe he'd introduce me to one of them, with the hope of making a case.

A few days later at the Miami office I met Marty, and after an exchange of greetings, he asked me some general questions as to where I was from and how long I had been an agent. Marty did not hold back with his questioning and went on to ask me if I had made any big cases in New York and against whom.

While I gave Marty some information as to where I was from and how long I'd been an agent, I also told him that it was none of his business who I had made cases on and the nature of the investigations, as that was confidential and I intended to keep it that way. I told Marty that this was not a good beginning, and he quickly apologized. Marty stated that he wasn't expecting me to violate confidentiality; he was just testing me out to see how I'd react. I told him that it wasn't necessary. If he wanted to see if I could hold my own, he would discover that once we hit the streets. I asked Marty if he was ready to go, and he asked me how much money I had. I asked him why, and he said that we'd probably meet some sharp guys and we would have to buy them drinks, etc. I told him I had enough and since we weren't going to be out all night, the money was not an issue.

We left the office and drove to a location by the Strip and parked. As we walked towards the Fontainebleau Lounge, we passed by an isolated street where there was a small group of men who appeared to be a mix of unemployed characters and street hustlers. Marty stopped and said, "Look, there's a guy in there I know has a lot of money on him. Let's roll him, and we'll have a little extra cash, okay?"

I said, "What did you say? Did I hear you correctly? Did you say, you wanted us to shake some guy down?"

"Yeah," he said. "It'll give us some extra bread for the evening, okay?"

"What, are you fucking crazy?" I hollered. "Listen, pal, I don't know what the fuck you're up to, but this isn't going to work. We're obviously starting off on the wrong foot."

I was completely baffled by what was happening, and I didn't know what had brought this on, so I asked him. "Listen, was this your idea, or did someone in the office plan this?"

Marty said, "No, no one in the office told me anything."

"So, this was your idea?" I asked.

"Yeah," he said, "I was just testing you out, man. I wanna make sure I'm working with the right guy."

"Listen pal," I said, "this is the second time you tried testing me. It seems to me that your idea of testing someone is to get them to do as you wish. Well, that's not going to work with me?"

Since I became an agent, I'd been working with informants at all levels, and the first thing you learn is not to trust them, and I wasn't about to trust this guy. Maybe he was wearing a wire, maybe this was an idea all his own or maybe someone put him up to it. Regardless, I was going to find out. So, I quickly said to him, "Now I'm going to test you, understand?"

"What do you mean?" he asked.

"I'm going to show you," I said. "Put your hands up against the wall and spread your legs."

"Why?" He asked.

"Because I'm gonna frisk you to see if you got drugs on you or to see if you're wired."

"You can't do this," he said.

"Listen," I said. "You just asked me to help you shake down that guy which is a crime. Now I want to make sure that there's no more crazy ideas or violations you might come up with like carrying a weapon or if you have any kind of drugs on you."

"Look, you can frisk me all you want. I don't have a weapon, nor do I have any drugs. And more important, I'm not wearing a wire, which is what you're really concerned about. Look, I'm sorry about what happened. It'll never happen again. Okay? I promise."

"Now listen to me, someone at the office said that you know some gamblers and drug dealers that you might be able to introduce me to, with the hope of making a case, and that's where I thought we were headed. But suddenly you come up with your own agenda that is the complete opposite of what I expected. And that's not happening, because, as of now, we're finished here. I'm calling it quits, and I'm heading back to the office."

"And by the way," I continued, "I'm gonna have to inform my supervisor why our original plan didn't work out and why I canceled the plan, so I'm leaving. You can do whatever the hell you want. I don't know what your relationship or status is with the office, but this incident isn't going to help you any."

Marty quickly suggested that I was overreacting. He was just trying to test me out because it's very hard and very dangerous to bring just anybody in to meet these guys. They're very sharp and very tough, and should they become aware of what he was up to, it would be the end for him, and he wasn't taking any chances.

I said to him, "Look, you obviously have a different agenda than I do. I don't subscribe to your philosophy, so this plan is not going to work. I suggest you tell whoever sent you to find someone else to work with, because as far as I'm concerned, we will not be working together. We're finished. Good-bye and good luck."

I returned to the office and informed my supervisor of what had transpired and informed them that if they still were interested in using this guy, they should consider someone else for the job. I never saw or heard from Marty again. I don't know if the incident had any relevancy or application to my transfer from New York to Miami, but it didn't matter and I didn't care. I was just looking forward to a better and more honest way to start.

23

Tijuana Investigation

Marcos Valdez - Jorge Favela Case

Pointing a .45 caliber handgun at my right temple, while simultaneously blowing smoke in my face after a puff from his cigar, the burly man with the swarthy complexion, in a heavy Mexican accent said, "My nephew says that you're a very nice guy and he likes you, and for now, that's good enough for me. But, if you look out the window towards the border, you see a hill, amigo. If I should find out that you're a Federale or Policia, I will blow your fucking head off and we'll bury you up on that hill where other Policias and Federales are buried." I remember those words vividly, and I will never forget them as long as I live.

All of this transpired on a hot and muggy early evening in February 1967 in Tijuana, Mexico. Those were the genuinely threatening words of Pablo Favela, who at the time was the biggest, if not one of the biggest, drug dealers in Tijuana. Words directed at me by Favela as we sat in the living room of his beautiful hacienda, getting acquainted and discussing price, quality, and quantity of cocaine I was considering buying.

Present in the room were Favela's two henchmen, Ricardo, who was sitting to Favela's left, and Tino, who was sitting to his right. I was seated in front of Favela, alongside his nephew Marcos Valdez, who had brought me there as his guest. This was to be an adventure right out of a Hollywood movie.

I had met Marcos Valdez a few weeks before in Miami. I had just returned from New York where I had gone to testify in a case that was brought to trial. Toward the end of the trial, I received a phone call from Bob Needham, supervisor of the Miami office, asking me if I could return to Miami ASAP.

A local cabdriver had apparently called the Miami office stating he had a fare he'd picked up, a Mexican male, who was looking for a customer for some cocaine he'd just brought from Tijuana. I agreed to get back as quickly as I could and proceeded to make arrangements and secured a flight that would arrive in Miami that night at about 9:00 PM. I agreed to meet Needham and the cab driver that evening about 9:30 PM at the main post office by the Miami Airport.

Upon arrival at the airport, I headed to the main post office where I met with Needham and a cab driver, whose name was Rudy Garcia. After the usual introductions, Needham left, and Garcia and I had a brief conversation. A journalism student who was putting himself through college by working as a cabbie, Garcia met Valdez when he picked him up as a fare and they began to get acquainted. Valdez, who spoke mostly Spanish, asked Garcia if he knew anyone who might be interested in buying high-grade, quality cocaine. As a good citizen doing his civic duty, Garcia brought the information to the attention of the Miami FBN office.

Garcia indicated that he would take me to Valdez, introduce me to him, but would then leave immediately as he had to go to work. Garcia also made it clear that he didn't want to be involved in any way, shape, or form with any investigation. Garcia and I then proceeded to a cocktail lounge at the Poinciana Hotel in Miami Springs where Valdez was staying. As soon as we met Valdez, Garcia quickly left our company, stating that he had to go to work.

Valdez and I exchanged greetings and had a brief conversation when I learned that his full name was Marcos Valdez and his uncle was Jorge Favela, one of the biggest drug dealers in Tijuana. His uncle had asked him for help in running the business because two of his best men were killed in an accident and there weren't many people that he could trust, especially in this line of work.

Valdez had been working very hard, so his uncle rewarded him by sending him on a vacation and telling him to have a good time while trying to broaden their market base by acquiring a couple of good customers. Valdez shared that he was looking for a couple of good, steady clients who would eventually buy large quantities of heroin or cocaine, which is what his uncle was more interested in.

I told Valdez I was originally from New York, but was now living in Miami. As a result, I had customers in both places, especially in the Hispanic community. And as I mentioned earlier, if the stuff was as good as he claimed, I'd be interested in buying real weight (kilo quantities). Valdez said he was happy to hear that and his uncle would be even happier to hear that another one of his clients was interested in buying kilo quantities.

I said to Valdez that if the cocaine was pure or top grade, and if I was going to spend that kind of bread buying a kilo or more, I wanted to know who I was dealing with.

In this case, I felt it was not only important, but a good business practice to meet with his uncle Favela, especially if I were going to consider buying large quantities from him and we were to continue to do business for a lengthy period of time.

Valdez stated that they also had marijuana, which he referred to as "Mexican Gold." He claimed it was better than "Panamanian Red," which at the time was very popular and known to be amongst the best marijuana around. I informed Valdez that I was more interested in cocaine and heroin than I was in marijuana.

I asked him how long he was going to be in town, and he said that he'd been gone a little longer than expected and was looking to head back to Tijuana by the end of the week, possibly Saturday. We had a couple of drinks and agreed to meet the following evening at about the same time.

The next day I informed Needham of what had transpired, and he was very pleased. I told him of the strong possibility of my going to Tijuana to meet Valdez's uncle, Jorge Favela, who was the source of supply for Valdez and was one of the biggest drug dealers in Mexico. I also indicated that this could be one of the biggest cases ever made in Miami.

When I questioned him about OAF, the money necessary for the purchase of cocaine, an enthusiastic Needham indicated that he would try to get approval for enough cash to buy a kilo of cocaine, but it wasn't going to be easy. When we have to leave the country and go to a place where we have no control of the situation, it's difficult to establish and conduct surveillance.

If he couldn't get approval for the money to buy a kilo, he would try to get approval for a much lesser amount. I explained to Needham that if I got to Tijuana and met with Favela and talked to him about buying a kilo or more without any money, I would really look bad. It would put me on the spot, and my credibility would be lost.

I had spent quite a bit of time with Valdez, and he'd begun to feel comfortable with me. We went to Miami Beach, stopping at some of the better known and more popular places in town, The Bolero, The Fontainebleau Cocktail Lounge, and Los Violines, a Cuban restaurant where they served authentic Cuban cuisine and the best in Latin dance music. Valdez, a gregarious type of individual, was a fun-loving guy who enjoyed fine food and a good time.

It was clear Valdez and I hit it off and had become better acquainted. He couldn't thank me enough for taking him to places he'd heard of, but had not been able to visit. In all our conversations, Valdez kept stressing the need to return to Tijuana, as he had been gone for some time and needed to get back. He felt very strongly that I'd be going with him and kept reminding me of the good time we were going to have. In fact, he made it clear that he'd definitely be returning to Tijuana on Saturday, which was a couple of days away, and he wanted to know if I was going with him. I told him I would let him know the next day.

The following morning I consulted with Needham about the pending trip. Before I got the opportunity to give him an update, he gave me the bad news. Much to my chagrin, they did not approve of the funds I was seeking to make a buy from one of the biggest drug dealers in Tijuana. I was shocked, to say the least. "Say what? Why?" I asked.

Needham indicated that he'd been talking to Washington, seeking approval for the purchase of a kilo or more of cocaine, but he'd gotten a negative response. In fact, those in command in Washington weren't even interested in pursuing the case, much less approving large amounts of money for purchasing drugs in places where we had no control of the situation.

I had no idea what was going on and couldn't understand why suddenly there was a lack of interest in a case with such huge potential. I didn't understand it. Just a few days ago, there was eagerness, enthusiasm, and a lot of support for the case that could be one of the biggest in Miami. I asked Needham for an explanation, but he was stymied. He didn't know what happened, but he was told that no funding whatsoever was being approved at this time, especially for a place like Tijuana. Even Needham seemed to agree with the decision, and I really could not understand that, particularly since he knew of the potential of the case, had expressed a lot of enthusiasm and was an early supporter of my pursuing the investigation.

I was extremely disappointed and completely baffled by what had just occurred. What was I going to tell Valdez? Everything was going so well, and then suddenly it was gloom and doom. I was dejected and depressed. It was a macabre type of feeling, resulting from what I felt was a very bad and dumb decision. Nonetheless, I had to deal with reality. So, I began to prepare myself as to what to tell Valdez.

I had passed myself off as a hotshot drug dealer, boasting about how I was going with him to Tijuana and buy large quantities of cocaine or heroin from his uncle, a major drug lord in Mexico. And now that it was time to back up my words, I didn't even have enough to buy a sample. Despite how awkward I felt, I had to come up with a plausible and convincing story that Valdez would believe and accept. By this time, I had begun to feel some animosity and bitterness towards my employers, and their attitude toward this case and the trip to Tijuana.

I went to meet with Valdez, and when I saw him, I told him that as eager as I was in going with him to Tijuana, serious family problems had surfaced that required my presence at home. At the same time, I had to come up with monies for some medical bills and legal fees my family was depending on. Therefore, any plans of going to Tijuana would have to be postponed. I apologized, but I did make it clear to him that the problem was temporary. As soon as I saw my way clear, I would contact him and buy the stuff as I intended. All I asked was for him to be patient and trust me.

Valdez, with a big smile on his face, surprisingly put his arm around my shoulder and said, "Don't worry about it, Amigo. You come to Tijuana with me. You be my guest. I'll pay for your round-trip fare, and if we're going to maintain a business relationship, I will add the cost of the trip to the cost of whatever you buy the first time, one or two kilos, whatever. But I want you to go with me to Tijuana. You're gonna love it. We're going to have a good time, I promise you."

I was very surprised at his response as it was totally unexpected. On the other hand, I was ecstatic, particularly after feeling so dejected and gloomy upon hearing of the disapproval of funds for the trip from Needham. "Will you be able to go?" asked Valdez.

I did not hesitate to answer. "Yes, I'm sure. I just have to take care of a few things at home and make some arrangements and last-minute preparations, but I'll be going with you."

I had made up my mind, right then and there, that I would go to Tijuana and pursue this investigation, no matter where it took me and regardless of the outcome. I obviously had to consult with my supervisor, but my mind was made up, and I didn't care what his reaction might be. Valdez stated that the flight leaves Saturday morning at 10:00 am from Miami Airport, so we could either leave together from the lobby of his hotel, or meet at the airport. Either way, I should let him know. I told him I'd meet him at the airport, since I had a few chores to run and some last-minute preparations.

24

Tijuana, Mexico

The next day I went to see Needham and informed him of what had transpired. He asked me what I was going to do, and I made it clear that I was going to Tijuana with Valdez. After all, I got a suspect to pay for my round-trip ticket to Tijuana, something that my own employers were not willing to do. "You can dispense with the sarcasm," Needham said. "Furthermore, it seems to me you're being spiteful and that that's why you're going."

"That's not true," I said. "I'm going because I want to develop this case and in view of the cast of characters, I want to build on it and make it the biggest case the Miami Office has ever made. Rarely do you have the opportunity to make a case against a drug dealer and his source of supply at the same time. Well, I have that opportunity, and I'm taking advantage of the situation."

Needham indicated that I should not go, stating that it was a bad idea on my part.

"Why?" I asked.

He said, "They declined to approve the OAF monies because they were not interested in pursuing the case, especially in a place like Tijuana where we would have no control of the situation. I don't think you should go, it's a bad idea."

I was angry but tried to hide my displeasure.

"Look," he said, "at this time, and for whatever the reason, the Bureau does not wish to pursue or support this case. Therefore, you'll have no money, no coverage or surveillance, and you're going into foreign soil. You'll be on your own in a very precarious and dangerous situation since the government has not approved any of this. So, I'm telling you, I don't think it's a good idea for you to go."

I explained to Needham that I'd made up my mind and I was going on a Saturday, my day off, so I would think the government couldn't tell me what to do or where to go in my spare time. Needham replied, "Don't push your luck. There's still the issue of insubordination, which will probably come up."

"Insubordination? Why?" I asked.

"Because you're disobeying orders, that's why."

"I'll take my chances," I said.

The flight Valdez and I were taking went straight from Miami to Los Angeles with a connecting flight to San Diego, California, at which time someone was picking us up and driving us to Tijuana. Truthfully I knew Needham's point was well taken. I had no coverage or surveillance, and although I didn't anticipate any problems during the flight, I thought someone else should be made aware of the trip in the event there were some unforeseen developments.

I called Artie Mendelsohn, a friend and an agent who used to be in New York but had been transferred to the Los Angeles office. I filled him in on the Tijuana investigation involving Valdez and Favela and gave him the flight information. We agreed to meet in the main lobby at the Los Angeles Airport upon my landing. Artie also pointed out that he had some contacts in the airline industry and would contact some key people to determine if there was anyone from Security on the flight. If so, the person assigned could maintain some degree of surveillance on me and Valdez during the flight to Los Angeles. I told Artie that I appreciated his concern and his cooperation, but I didn't think that would be necessary. Artie stated that he'd look into it anyway.

In the meantime, I also called Larry Katz, the agent in charge of the San Diego office. I filled him in and also gave him the flight information. Larry said that once we landed in San Diego, he was fairly certain that Valdez would have someone pick us up and drive us to the San Diego/Tijuana border. Larry stated that he would maintain surveillance once we landed in San Diego, but that would probably end once we got to the border. From that point on, I'd be on my own as all surveillance would terminate. Since he would not be able to conduct surveillance beyond the border, Katz gave me his contact number and told me to call him regardless of the situation.

Valdez and I left Miami as scheduled, and approximately five hours later we landed at the LA Airport. During the flight, we had a drink and a little of the usual flight food. We also took a nap and talked for a while. Valdez briefly told me that his uncle would probably grow angry with him for bringing me to his home, his hacienda. His uncle Favela had always told him that he should never bring strangers to the house, regardless who.

However, Valdez said that I should not be concerned because he had no regrets having me as his guest. But he warned me that his uncle often gets annoyed and angry when things don't go his way. Valdez wanted me to know that his uncle can be very intimidating and threatening in certain situations. But he told me not to worry, as he would not let his uncle get out of hand and that I should not be concerned.

Upon landing at the Los Angeles Airport, we had a one-hour wait before the connecting flight, and Valdez went to make a phone call. I walked slowly around the main lobby and spotted my friend, Agent Artie Mendelssohn. I headed towards the men's room and Artie followed. Once inside, we hugged and embraced, during which time he asked me how the flight was and if everything was okay. I told him the flight was good and everything was going according to plan. We conferred briefly on the case, and he proceeded to give me his number and said I should call him should the need arise, regardless of the circumstances. Artie hung around the airport until it was time to board for the flight to San Diego.

We boarded the next plane and approximately one hour later landed at San Diego Airport. As we reached the luggage area, I saw my other friend Agent Larry Katz, nearby. After retrieving the luggage, Valdez and I walked towards the street where we were greeted by a Latino male who hugged Valdez and welcomed him home. Valdez introduced him to me as Ricardo, an old friend of the family. We got into a station wagon that was being driven by another Latino male who was introduced to me as Tino, also an old friend of the family. We exchanged greetings, and Tino asked Valdez in Spanish about the flight. As we drove away, Valdez and the two men got into a conversation in Spanish. While they spoke, I looked at the rear view mirror and noticed Larry Katz following us in his vehicle.

When we got to the border, we stopped to answer a few questions by border police and then continued on our way. I looked in the rear view mirror again, but I saw that Larry was no longer following us as he'd mentioned. From that point on, I was truly on my own.

The driver indicated that he was taking a shortcut to Favela's home. The road we were riding on was all dirt, rocky and bumpy. Riding in the station wagon I felt like I needed a saddle. And the area we were passing through was a mountainous and desolate region, reminding me of a town in the Old West.

As we got near Favela's home, we stopped at a motel, where I was staying. After checking in, Valdez told me that it was their policy to search all visitors to check their ID and determine if they're carrying any weapons. Ricardo searched my person, while Tino searched my luggage. They found nothing that was of value to them. All I had was a bogus

ID under the name of "Bobby Cubano," the name I used for undercover purposes. After the search, we drove to Favela's home, a beautiful hacienda by a lake with a couple of German Shepherds and a few cats in the backyard. We entered the house, and I was instructed to make myself comfortable in the living room where we'd gathered. Valdez indicated that we were going to have dinner and then asked the group what they were drinking. He offered me some tequila emphasizing that it was the best tequila in Mexico. I respectfully declined and requested instead a "Johnny Walker Black". My request was granted. As we sat in the living room, I was again offered some "Tequila," but I indicated that my preference for scotch.

A short time later, Favela entered the living room dressed in a green fatigue outfit with a matching cap like Fidel Castro. Wearing what appeared to be an expensive gold watch and a chain around his neck, Favela, a burly man with a swarthy complexion and a mustache, walked towards us, smoking and blowing the smoke into the air until he got to where we were standing.

Favela, who spoke English with a heavy Mexican accent, greeted all present and then hugged and embraced his nephew Marcos Valdez, who immediately introduced me to his uncle. Valdez explained to him that I was the guy he had been talking about, whom he'd invited to be his guest. We exchanged greetings, and Favela, blowing smoke at my face, asked me where I was from. I told him I was originally from New York, but I had recently moved to Miami to be close to family and look over family business interests. Favela, repeating himself, said, "Like I said, Marcos likes you and speaks well of you. He also told me you're interested in buying some "material" to take back to the states. I nodded in agreement and told him that for starters I was interested in buying a kilo of cocaine, maybe more, depending on the quality of the stuff. Favela went on to say, "Well, let me ask you, how much money do you have?

Fifteen thousand, ten thousand?"

I said, "To be honest with you senor, I just have some spending money. I don't have enough money to buy any drugs at all. But, I'll have the money when I'm ready to buy. I really came down as Marcos's guest to meet you senor, and to check out the prices, and the quality of the stuff."

"You mean to tell me that you don't have enough money to buy even one kilo? And you are from New York and Miami, real fancy places and you don't have any fucking money. I don't think that was a good idea, amigo."

I could tell that Favela was not thrilled with the idea that his nephew had brought over a potential customer from a place like Miami and New York and the guy doesn't have any money. The situation did not sit well with him and it aroused suspicion.

Favela walked towards me and blowing smoke from his cigar in my face, in his harsh and threatening tone of voice, said, "You, Senor, have some pair of "COJONES," coming here and talking a whole lot of bullshit and making like a big shot without any fucking money. You are very lucky that Marcos likes you and says you're okay. Marcos is family, and I trust him. And, he's a very happy-go-lucky guy who makes friends easy and loves to have a good time. But sometimes he forgets that this is a very serious and dangerous business, so I have to often remind him."

Favela then pulled out a .45 caliber pistol from a desk drawer nearby, and pointed it right at my temple said, "I just wish to remind you senor, that if we should find out you're a Federale or Policia, I will blow your fucking head off and bury you with the rest of your comrades up on the hill." He stopped to point to a hill by the border. "You understand that?"

"Yes, I do, Senor. Very well," I said.

Despite not having the money to buy the drugs, I was getting a bit annoyed with his cowboy mentality, his intimidating ways, and the threatening manner in which he spoke to me.

There was however validity to what he said, so I could understand how he felt. His nephew Marcos, knowing that he does not want people brought to the house, especially strangers, shows up with some guy from Miami who's talking about buying a whole lot of shit but has no money. The guy doesn't have enough money to buy a smaller quantity or even a sample of the stuff. That would make anyone angry.

But, by the same token, I couldn't let him continue to intimidate me. I had to let him know I didn't appreciate being spoken to that way. I was not a pushover, nor was I going to be bullied. After all I'm a drug dealer from New York and Miami. Therefore I had to act like one even if I was in 'enemy' territory. I was thinking in my attempts to make the case I may have lost some objectivity and created a deep hole for myself. Maybe Needham was right; maybe I should have dropped the case or taken a different path. Besides, what about respect? Was I going to let his uncle bully me around? On the spot I made up my mind there was no way that was going to happen, yet it appeared to heading that way. Moreover, what did Valdez think of what was going on, and what did he really think about me? He himself had told me not to be too concerned with his uncle, but I couldn't let them think I was some kind of a pushover or a wimp.

I was in a quandary. It seemed like a dual dilemma, if there was such a thing. I left Miami in a wave of controversy surrounding this investigation, especially the trip to Tijuana. I was told not to make the trip, but I did anyway, disobeying orders and that translates into insubordination.

Now, I was in Tijuana, with the main suspect whom I had become friendly with and his uncle, who was a drug lord and more importantly, the source of supply. But, I also found myself without funds, and at that particular moment, without a gun, while Favela kept waving a .45 by my temple. No money and no gun! The only weapon I had left was myself, my mouth and the ability to defend myself. I had come so far in such a short period of time, but Favela was right. I didn't even have enough money to buy a sample, and reputable drug-dealers do not walk around broke or empty handed.

I had come so far in such a short period of time. If everything turned out well, the investigation had the potential to become one of the biggest, if not the biggest, case ever made in Miami. I certainly didn't want to blow the opportunity.

The situation at the Miami office was another issue still in the back of my mind. It appeared that the people in charge were no longer interested. Nevertheless, that would have to wait until I returned. First things first, and one step at a time.

In order to make a case against Favela, I needed to maintain a solid business relationship with the man. If there was anything that could negatively affect that outcome, I felt compelled to take the initiative and prevent that from happening. I had to clear the air and set the record straight. I had to say something that would make Favela feel comfortable with me being there and, at the same time, gain his confidence so that he looked forward to doing business with me, if not now, certainly in the very near future.

Equally as important, I had to make certain that he understood that I was not going to be intimidated, not even by a drug kingpin with a .45 caliber pistol being pointed at my head.

Bringing me there had been a mistake on Valdez's part, because he knew it was against his uncle's wishes. But if I expected to make this case, I would have to negotiate and deal with the big man himself. He was not a happy camper, and I wasn't exactly in his good graces. Therefore, I had to make him understand that things were not as he perceived them. And there was nothing for him to be upset or concerned about. I had to address the issues and present myself as someone he could feel comfortable with and do business with. I also wanted to convince him that his nephew Valdez did the right thing by bringing me there, as I would be a long-term customer. The fact of the matter was that I created the problem and I would have to fix it. Everything had been going so well, when suddenly the bottom fell out. It was time to clear the air and set the record straight, so I approached Favela and asked him if we could talk in private. He complied with my request, and we moved to an adjoining room where it was just the two of us.

25

Confrontation

"Look, Mr. Favela," I said, "I'm on my way back home, but before I leave, I would like to clear the air since there seems to be some sort of misunderstanding about my being here and the purpose of my visit. More important is the fact that based on what Marcos told me, I intended to buy a kilo or more of cocaine, yet I don't even have enough money to buy an ounce or even a sample."

"First of all, I want to thank both you and Marcos for letting me be your guest and for your hospitality. Now, if you honestly and sincerely feel I'm a Federale or a Policia, then go ahead, blow my fucking brains out. But, understand one thing, I'm not afraid of you nor anyone else and pointing a .45 at my head is not going to solve any problems. Besides, I've dealt with many weapons in the past, heavy weapons while in the Army and hand guns and other types like yours with mob guys in New York. So, let's get this straight, guns don't scare me. Now, I know I'm on foreign soil. But regardless where I am, I treat people the way I want to be treated, and that is with respect."

I continued. "Now, you mentioned earlier that you didn't like the idea of Marcos bringing me here because you prefer doing business with your close circle of friends. I don't blame you for being angry and upset, because this is a very dangerous business and you should only deal with people you know and trust. Well,

I'm the same way. But, as you probably know, sometimes you know people all of your life and you can trust them as far as you can throw them. Then, there are some people that you know for a short period of time and you trust them implicitly."

"I'm sure you're also aware that to be successful in business, you have to take risks. And both you and Marcos took a risk in bringing me here. Marcos took a risk with me in Miami and he can tell you that if I were a Federale or Policia, I would have locked him up in Miami. But let me tell you why I'm here and why I have no money."

I was on a roll and I knew he was listening. "As I told you, I'm from New York, now living in Miami; I can assure you, there's a big market in both places for cocaine, heroin and marijuana, particularly the one you boast about. I have clients in both Miami and New York and although I can get the stuff over there, it's probably not as good as yours. That's why I need a good, reliable source of supply. I'm very interested in buying a kilo for starters, and, depending on the quality and price, I'll continue to buy more. So, if you can provide me with quality stuff at a reasonable price, you will have a steady customer."

"Now, as to why I don't have any money. I met Marcos a couple of weeks ago while he was in Miami. We had a few drinks, and then went out to dinner and started to get acquainted. I took him to a few places I'm familiar with and we had a great time. In fact, Marcos and I hit it off right away and when I learned that he was from Tijuana and the stuff came from Mexico, I was really enthused. I told him I was really interested in buying a kilo or more, depending on the quality and the price. Marcos then said that if I really wanted to buy large quantities of stuff it would probably be better if I came here to Tijuana."

"At the time, quite frankly, I probably had enough money to buy a quarter or a half kilo, which was my original intention. But some family problems and health issues came up, not to mention legal fees that I had to pay my attorney. And that left me short of money. Frankly, I did not want to embarrass myself, and I didn't want to appear as someone that takes advantage of people. I explained to Marcos the reasons why I couldn't make the trip and therefore, I would have to postpone it temporarily."

I watched his eyes and knew he was still with me. "But Marcos, being the kind of person he is, told me not to worry, that he wanted me to be his guest in Tijuana. He said he would pay for my round-trip fare, and while I was excited, I told him he didn't have to do that. Marcos went on to say, that if I felt uncomfortable about not paying for the fare, he would add the cost of the fare to the cost of whatever I bought from you the first time. And by the way, that was a clever move by Marcos, from a business stand-point that is."

"Bringing me here as a guest, and then adding the cost to the price of whatever I bought, that was a very smart move. On the one hand, he kept his potential client happy, while at the same time, the client would pay for the trip when the sale went through. That is a good tactic in business. Clearly, Marcos knew what he was doing. So here we are. And that, Senor, is basically how this all came about."

"Now," I continued, "let me just say that there's a window of opportunity here for a good, healthy business relationship. I would like very much to do business with you, and I promise you, I'll be back soon. However, if you still feel that you want to blow my fucking brains out, then go ahead and do what you must. All I can tell you is that I'm not a fucking pushover, and I don't frighten easily. I've dealt with some mob guys who are tough and dangerous and they don't all carry forty fives, but they carry different types of guns."

"Here in Tijuana you are a well-known hombre with a fine reputation and I respect that. But I treat people the way I want to be treated. I have done nothing, nor will I do anything, to disrespect you and frankly, I'm anxious to come back and do business with you. But, if you still have doubts about me and you don't want to do business with me, then Senor Favela, you'll never see me again. I would like to thank you and Marcos once again for allowing me to be your guest and thank you for your hospitality and for taking the time. I look forward to doing business with you real soon. And as they say in Spanish, 'Muchisimas gracias y encantado en haberle conocido' (which translates to "Thank you very much, it's been a pleasure meeting you.).")

I've portrayed many roles working undercover, but I don't recall any that required or included a "Soliloquy." Such bravado can be foolish or dangerous. I may have dramatized the message I delivered to Favela, but I felt compelled to do so. I felt relieved as I couldn't leave there without getting a few things off my chest, especially since I was supposed to be a drug-dealer from New York/Miami.

In the interim, I was hoping that the commentary had not angered him. After all, Favela was still the one holding the gun. However, I must have struck a nerve, or perhaps it was just plain luck. As I went to shake hands with him, Favela also made a gesture to shake hands, but instead, he embraced and hugged me.

Favela then stated, "Well, Mr. Bobby Cubano, that was a good speech. Marcos was right, you are a nice person Amigo, but more important, you have personality, you have character, and you are very fucking brazen. And I love brazen. I had said to you before, you have some pair of cojones, coming here with intentions of buying a kilo or more of cocaine or heroin, but you have no fucking money. Now, you are leaving but you want to get some shit off your chest and you approach me knowing how I feel. That takes a lot of guts, but I like people with "COJONES." You also seem to be very honest and sincere by what you have said. I am really, really impressed by your honest talk, Amigo. Now, let's eat and go for a few drinks and by the way, I want you to try the tequila here in Tijuana. It's the best in Mexico and Mexico has the greatest tequila in the world, so you will not be disappointed."

After dinner, we went out to a local club for drinks and to listen to good music. We heard a "Mariachi" band that was excellent and then a Latin group came on and played very good dance music. Valdez had told his uncle about my dancing and Favela quickly called the club manager over and after a brief conversation. We were joined at the table by a very personable and attractive young woman. Favela went on to say, "Since Marcos tells me you're a very good dancer, and you are from New York and Miami. I want to see how well you can do against our best. Margarita here is the best in Tijuana."

After an exchange of greetings, Margarita and I danced a Mambo and a Cha-Cha that went over very well. She was very good and I complemented her dancing and told her she could compete against anyone. When I asked her if she could Tango, she said no. Thus, as fine a dancer as she was, Margarita would have a difficult time competing against the New York gals who normally include the tango in their dance routine. Being from New York, I was obviously articulating my biases.

Favela returned the compliment and told me that Marcus was right about me as a person and a dancer. Margarita remained at the table, had some food, a couple of drinks and then left to join her group. After a fine enjoyable evening of great food and drink, we went home.

The following morning, I thanked Valdez for all he'd done and thanked his uncle Favela for his hospitality. I made it clear to him that the next time, we would do business for certain and I would be prepared to purchase a kilo of cocaine, possibly more.

Favela said, "When you come back and I hope that's very soon, I will give you that big package I've been promoting for free. I've been promoting it because it's the best marijuana you ever tasted or you could find anywhere. We keep hearing that in places like Chicago, New York, and Miami, the best marijuana is Panamanian Red or Chicago Green. Well, they are nothing compared to the Mexican Gold I'm going to give you when you come back and that's on me."

I would like to think that even notorious drug lords possess or can display some form of decency or be a part of the human element.

After what we'd been through, it was apparent that Favela was less hostile and a bit more understanding. Given what he said, I think I was on the right path. But, he wasn't going to let me forget who he really was as he repeated his earlier comments, "Listen, Amigo, we've had a lot of fun and I hope we do business, a lot of business.

But let me be very clear on something that is very real down here, and I repeat, very real. If we were to find out you were a Federale or a Policia, I will personally blow your fucking head off and bury you with all the other Federales and Policias up on the hill, you understand? Let me be very clear senor. I don't say that to be a tough hombre, it's just a reminder, that's just the way we do things down here."

To be perfectly clear, Favela repeated the same message in Spanish and then ended our conversation with his usual politeness. "Muchas gracias y que lleve buen viaje. Espero verle pronto," which means, "Thank you, have a good trip Hope to see you soon."

26

Confusion and Frustration

Now that some of the tension and friction in Tijuana had subsided, the aim was to effect changes in Miami by trying to renew interest in this investigation and resurrect the case. When I returned to Miami, I informed Needham of what had transpired in Tijuana. I made him aware of my relationship with Valdez and Favela, and the opportunity to still develop this case to its fullest. It had the potential to be not just an excellent case but the biggest ever in the Miami office.

Although Needham seemed satisfied with what transpired in Tijuana, he did not appear to be as enthused as when I first met Valdez He stated that it was more important that I had returned home safe and sound. But, he added, there was good news and bad hews he wanted to share with me. Needham stated that the good news was that there would not be any further talk of insubordination, as it was now a non-issue.

With regard to the investigation, because of the passion I had for the case and the effort I had put into it, he'd conferred with the people in Washington and had succeeded in keeping the case open. The bad news was that I had to surrender the case to the Los Angeles Office.

Upon hearing that, I asked, "What? Why?" His response was that in terms of control, the L.A. office had the manpower and the resources to maintain better control of the case, particularly since the bulk of the work in the investigation would be in Tijuana. And, from a logistics standpoint, I had to agree.

"But don't get angry or upset, Needham kept saying, "you will get due credit for the initiation of the case and, depending on the outcome, you will receive appropriate recognition."

"That's very nice," I said, "but that's not what I was looking for. I've been handling the case all along and I could control the situation because I've been to Tijuana and I know the players. In fact, I have a very good relationship with the suspect [Valdez] as well as the source of supply, his uncle [Favela], something none of the people in Los Angeles have. And that's key. After all, whoever gets the case will have to start from scratch and, depending on who the undercover agent is, it could mean the difference between success and failure."

"That's true," Needham said, "but from a logistics standpoint, they're better situated and have better resources to handle the case."

"I would say," Needham added, "that as of this moment, that's their biggest concern. I'm sure when the time comes they'll get the right undercover agent. Look, with your knowledge of the case and given your relationship with both Valdez and Favela, you can help to facilitate the process of initiating and developing this case to its fullest potential."

"I understand all that," I said. "I just thought that since I've had the case from the very beginning, I would be allowed to continue."

"Listen," Needham added, "consider yourself fortunate. It was touch and go regarding the issue of insubordination. And don't worry, you will receive your share of credit for the case, all right. But you've got to forget this whole thing and go on, okay?"

I was not a happy camper. I had put in a lot of time and effort on the case, risked my own life and now I had to turn it over. Suddenly I found myself isolated, disinterested, and uninspired, fighting with a total desire to withdraw. Since I was sworn in, I'd had nothing but great feelings and a very positive attitude towards this job, but the eagerness and enthusiasm I'd always had suddenly began to wane.

I prepared a report that included an outline and update on the investigation and sent it to the L.A. office, advising them that the case was being referred to them for appropriate action, but I would be available for consultation.

At the time of this investigation, most FBN offices had a telephone in the office to be used for undercover purposes only (undercover telephone conversations, messages, etc.).

One afternoon, several weeks after the case was referred, the undercover telephone in the Miami office rang and I picked it up. The caller asked for "Bobby Cubano," at which time I became suspicious and asked who was calling. The caller discreetly identified himself as Tony Martinez and began telling me that he was an agent in the Los Angeles office, working undercover on the Valdez/Favela investigation.

Martinez filled me in on what had transpired since the agency had forwarded the case to his office. He said he was assigned to the case and he'd approached Valdez a couple of times to try and make a buy from him. Although Valdez was reluctant, when my name came up, Valdez seemed to be more willing to deal. They negotiated for the purchase of a kilo of heroin and at that particular moment, he found himself in conflict with Valdez. Martinez stated that he couldn't fill me in on all the details because he was faced with time constraints and he didn't want to raise suspicion as to who we both were.

However, Martinez stated that he'd been negotiating with Valdez for a kilo of heroin for $15,000. Although everything seemed to be going well, Valdez wanted the money out front and he would go pick up the kilo of heroin and deliver it to Martinez by a warehouse where both had agreed to meet. Martinez, on the other hand, was under strict orders that under no circumstances was he was to front the money. The two men were arguing the issue of fronting the money, and had reached a stalemate. Martinez then suggested to Valdez that he would call "Bobby Cubano" to see how he might help.

"Why me?" I asked.

"Because," Martinez stated, "Valdez likes you and is always talking about you, his friend Bobby Cubano from Miami and New York."

Since he frequently asked about me, Martinez figured that by bringing me into the picture, Valdez would be glad to talk to me. In the interim, I could also try to exercise my influence in favor of Martinez, so he wouldn't have to front the money. Hopefully, Valdez's attitude would change and they could bring the deal to fruition.

I thought quickly about it, and despite my feelings about having to turn the case over to the L.A. office, I couldn't leave a fellow agent in a perilous situation. I told Martinez to put Valdez on the phone. I had to think fast and explain why had I not called him, and what happened to our deal? Was I no longer interested?

When Valdez got on the phone, we exchanged greetings, at which time Valdez asked me what happened. He wanted to know why I hadn't called him to let him know when I'm coming down to Tijuana? I explained to Valdez that nothing had changed in my personal or family life, but I found myself with serious financial problems. I said, "Because money remains an issue, I didn't want to go to Tijuana and embarrass myself, especially after that conversation your uncle and I had before I left. But, not to worry, my problems have eased somewhat, and I should be going down within a couple of weeks, so I'll be calling you and I thank you for your concern."

"But listen Marcos," I went on, "take care of my friend [Antonio] and I guarantee you'll be able to get rid of a few more kilos. His boss is an old friend of mine, and I'll call him immediately and tell him that you and I are friends and how you've helped me out in the past."

I could tell he was listening, "Look, the kid is under orders not to front the money because they don't know who you are, and they're always afraid of what could happen to the money, particularly when you don't know who you're dealing with. If it were me, I would give you the money because I know you and trust you."

Valdez said, "Well, if that's true, why don't you convince him by telling him that you and I are friends and I can be trusted."

"Well, I'm going to," I said, "but after this deal. The reason I won't tell him now is because he's got the money. I'm sure you've already determined that he's got the $15,000 in an attaché case, no? You've already seen the money, correct? And you've got the drugs, and you know where they are. He doesn't. I'm sure you're aware that you've got the edge. Besides, he's in your territory. You've got your people all over the place. It would be like committing suicide for him to try and do something stupid. Whereas, you know the money's there, you've seen it, and you're in possession of the drugs which he doesn't know."

After a brief pause I continued, "If I were in his shoes, and I didn't know you, I'd probably do the same thing. So, try to understand his situation. But look, that's neither here nor there. It's a question of trust, and the difference is I know you and I trust you, and I know you feel the same. I believe you're going to get the stuff and bring it to him. He's going to pay you the exact amount you guys agreed to for the kilo, whatever the total price is, and everything is going to work out fine. Okay?"

"My friend," he said, "you have a way of dealing with people. Even my uncle [Jorge Favela] said that. He told me that right after you left. 'Marcos,' he said, 'your friend seems to me to be one of those slick guys from New York who know how to bullshit people.'"

"Well, look," Valdez stated, "I'm going to do it, but only because you asked me to and I hope to see you soon, okay? But, listen, this will be the first and last time I do it. The next time, it will be either my way or the highway, okay. Understood, my friend? As a matter of fact, I'm going to tell him that."

"Remember," I said, "he's a young guy who's following orders. He's also worried that someone will take advantage of him. Now I know you wouldn't do that, but he's afraid that you won't return, so he's somewhat apprehensive. Treat him right, because you'll be doing me a favor. But, trust me, go get the shit and bring it to the kid, and I'll see to it that you are taken care of when it's all over. Okay? And in addition, when I come down, I'll make it up to you. But, do me a favor, go get the stuff and make sure he's getting good quality shit. Take care of the kid as if he were me. Okay?"

Valdez said, "Okay, my friend, I'll take care of him, but you ask me to treat him like I would treat you. Well, he's not you. I'm not sure about him. I don't like him, and he makes me nervous. He came here to see me and he wants very much to meet my uncle, but I told him that's not going to happen. Why? And if he continues to bug me about meeting my uncle, I will not do business with him. If he keeps pestering me, maybe I will introduce him to my uncle. And I'll have my uncle intimidate him or threaten him like he did you. Remember? I would like to see the expression on his face when my uncle tells him that if he finds out he's a Federale or Policia, he'll blow his fucking brains out and bury him with his compadres. I'd love to see his reaction."

I could hear some of Valdez's concerns coming through so I didn't interrupt. "He must think I'm going to take his money and disappear. Well, I don't need his fucking money. The only reason he's still here is that he mentioned he wanted to talk to you to prove to me he's okay. I went along with it because it would give me a chance to talk to you and see how you're doing. And if you say he's okay, that's fine with me. Now, let me tell you, I'm very disappointed that you don't even call me. I expect to see you soon. All right?"

"Yes," I said, "I promise I'll call you and if you take care of this kid today I'll make sure you get more business from them. Okay? Marcos, it's been great talking to you. I will see you soon, and I promise I'll call. Now put the kid back on the phone."

When Martinez returned to the phone, I explained to him that he wouldn't have to front the money, but to be careful, nevertheless. I told him if he's been negotiating with Valdez, to make certain he deals only with Valdez and hold him accountable if he doesn't bring him the exact amount or if he tries to get slick and change plans at the last minute. Martinez couldn't thank me enough. But I could detect that he was nervous. Needless to say, he was faced with time constraints and was very nervous as Valdez was nearby or close enough perhaps to hear some of the conversation.

Furthermore, the reality was that it was two federal narcotic agents having an undercover conversation concerning the purchase of a kilo of heroin and the main suspect or player was alongside of him. I told Martinez to keep me posted and I wished him the best of luck. He thanked me again, stating that he would call me.

A week went by, and he didn't call. I felt awkward calling there and inquiring about the case that I had referred, so I decided to call my friend Mendelsohn who had greeted me at the airport when I traveled with Valdez on the way to Tijuana.

Mendelsohn stated that it had been kept hush, hush, but it was no secret that someone botched the case as plans had gone wrong. The two main guys got away, and they arrested the delivery man who was driving a station wagon and some flunky they had brought along. They also seized one kilo of heroin and a fairly large amount of marijuana. But, word around the office was, there were last-minute negotiations for a few kilos of heroin and plans went awry.

Notwithstanding the outcome of the case, the most important thing was that no one was hurt or injured. And I was not about to second-guess anyone, nor was I going to take a disparaging view towards the person who screwed up the case. We all make mistakes, and things don't always go as planned.

Nevertheless, I had some concerns as to how the case was handled, and I felt very strongly that I would probably have handled things much differently. My biggest disappointment was that I was never given the opportunity to officially make the case against Valdez or Favela.

I was quite disheartened because, for all intents and purposes, I had initiated the case against the two men. I had met the suspect as well as his source of supply. I had been negotiating with the source of supply (a drug lord) for purchases of large quantities of drugs. The only thing missing was the evidence (drugs), which I could not purchase because I had no money.

Despite the results of the case and the fact that my enthusiasm and eagerness seemed to have waned, I continued to do my job as expected, albeit not with the same fervor or desire.

27

Transfer to New Orleans

Subsequent to the Tijuana case, as we approached the Christmas season in Miami (1967), I received notification that once again I was being transferred, this time to New Orleans. The news hit me like a ton of bricks. It was déjà vu all over again. I couldn't believe this was happening to me. It was like the old adage, 'One step forward and two steps backwards.'

Once again, I was shocked by news that arrived without any form of explanation. But this time I was beginning to feel the psychological effects. I was a nervous wreck. If the transfer to Miami was a disappointment, the transfer to New Orleans was painful. It was disturbing, gut-wrenching, and surreal. Why was I being transferred to New Orleans?

Although the transfer to Miami had made no sense at the time as there was a huge influx of Cubans into Miami after the Castro takeover, coupled with the fact that there were no Spanish-speaking agents in the office. Although I was not ecstatic about the idea, it was a scenario that I was prepared to accept. In that case, perhaps I overreacted. But, a transfer to New Orleans, Why? I was just starting to get acquainted with Miami, the town and its people. I couldn't understand it. I was baffled, astonished. I was also beginning to wonder if I was being treated differently. Was I being held to a different standard?

When you work undercover, you depend and rely a lot on your instincts, your gut feelings, and both my instincts and gut feelings were telling me that something was wrong. I was going crazy. I thought I was suffering from some form of psychosis or paranoia. Ever since I left New York, things had not gone as well as I expected. Just as I start to get acquainted with Miami and the office personnel, two inexplicable incidents occurred, both of which were never truly addressed or fully explained. And both left me dumbfounded.

First of all, there was the 'shakedown' incident with the informant. I met him just once, and during that first meeting he wanted me to join him in shaking down someone in an alley. Was that coincidental, or was that by design? Was someone trying to set me up? If so, why?

Following that incident, I had occasion to meet Marcos Valdez, a Mexican drug dealer, whose uncle, Jorge Favela, was the source of supply and a drug lord from Tijuana. After gaining his confidence, he took me as his guest to Tijuana to meet the uncle.

The investigation had the potential to be one of the biggest cases ever initiated in Miami, but suddenly my request for money (OAF) to make drug purchases was declined. Additionally, the case was taken away from me, and I was asked to turn the case over to the Los Angeles office for logistical reasons. In both instances, the question I'd kept asking myself was, Why?

Now, suddenly I was faced with a transfer to New Orleans. I asked Needham if he knew anything about the transfer, and he said no. I called New York and asked Ben Fitzgerald, and he didn't know. No one knew anything. I was at a loss for words.

Moreover, in seeking sympathy or support, there was very little, if any, because most people felt the same way about New Orleans as they did about Miami. After all, both Miami and New Orleans were great cosmopolitan towns with great restaurants, great music, and great sports teams. Even my own friends were telling me that both towns offered all the things I truly enjoyed, so what the hell was I upset about? However, it wasn't the same. Unfortunately, I began to feel all alone. Whenever I inquired for reasons or asked questions, the response was the same. The government does not have to explain the reasons why, that comes with the territory, and you knew that coming in, so just accept it.

It reminded me of my early days in the Army. When I finished basic training in New Jersey, I was given orders that I was headed to Korea without any explanation, just orders from the government. I remembered asking my sergeant why we were being sent to Korea and not Europe or Panama where other soldiers were being shipped to. And in his heavy Southern accent, he quickly asked me, "Where are you from, Gonzalez?"

"New York, Sergeant."

"What part of New York, boy?"

"Brooklyn, Sergeant."

"Well, boy, I got good news for you. They're sending all you guys from Brooklyn to Korea, so you won't be alone, you'll have plenty of company. You understand? So, grin and bear it. You hear me, soldier?"

"Yes, sir," I said.

"And don't call me sir. I work for a living. You hear me, boy?"

"Yes, Sergeant!" I shouted.

"Now, start packing, boy."

Well, like a good soldier, I followed orders and did what I was told.

I didn't know why all this had been bothering me so much, but I knew something was wrong. I made up my mind to try and find out. I needed to sit down in a quiet place and do some meditation, introspection, etc. and try, to the extent that I could, to figure things out for myself. Maybe I was making too much out of all this. But I needed a break. I needed to go someplace quiet where I could relax and meditate.

I decided to take a few days off before reporting to New Orleans, which would give me some time to relax and think. I had a good friend in New York who had a ranch house in Vero Beach, Florida.

Perhaps a few days at the ranch house would help me clear my mind.

Manny Garcia, an elderly gentleman from Cuba, was a successful businessman in the shipping container business in New Jersey. Manny was a great supporter of law enforcement, and I had been instrumental in making him an "Honorary Sheriff" in Westchester County, New York. Besides his home in Yonkers, New York, Manny had this ranch house in Vero Beach, Florida, where he spent his free time and vacationed with his family. He was also a horse owner, and the ranch house had a barn and a training track for his horses.

I called Manny and explained to him that I was on my way to New Orleans on official business and I was driving there from Miami. Because it was a long trip, I could use a couple of days of rest and relaxation, and I asked him if he wouldn't mind some company. He stated that he'd be delighted to see me and said he was going to be at the ranch over the holidays with his family. He asked me to spend a few days with them at the ranch and ring in the New Year, which I agreed to do. I thought it would be a great idea to spend the holidays with a friend, while at the same time I would be able to relax, think, and try to make some sense out of all this.

We had a wonderful time and celebrated New Year's Eve, which helped to ease some of the stress I had begun to feel. I enjoyed my stay very much, and after a couple of days, expressed my gratitude to my friend and set forth on my long drive to the FBN office in New Orleans, my new headquarters.

New Orleans as a port is well located geographically to serve as a distribution center of drugs for other countries in South and

Central America. It is similar to New York and Miami, as it is also known for its round-the-clock night life, vibrant live music, and its great food, including its famous ethnic cuisine.

Located by the famous French Quarter, the FBN office was similar to the Miami office, as it had about the same number of agents and a secretary. The agent in charge was Jim Bland.

As in Miami, the office had a good working relationship with the local police, especially the Narcotics Squad of the New Orleans Police Department.

After my arrival, I spent a few weeks familiarizing myself with office policy and procedures and reviewing files on pending cases and updates on fugitives.

While simultaneously becoming acquainted with the other agents, I made a few cases. Inasmuch as I was still trying to figure out why I had been transferred there, it was clear to me that the need for a Spanish-speaking agent in New Orleans was a non-issue. It was quite apparent there was no urgency there. I couldn't figure out what I was doing there, but that quickly changed.

28

Mississippi Pilots Investigation
New Orleans, Louisiana

One cold, windy afternoon in February 1968, shortly after my transfer to New Orleans, the phone in the office rang. There was no one in the office at the time, not even the secretary, so I answered the phone. The caller, a male individual, asked to speak to an agent because he had crucial information concerning narcotics being brought into this country. I told him I was an agent, and he asked if there was any way I could meet him as soon as possible. I asked why, and he quickly stated that both he and his friend were pilots from the Mississippi area and they were about to fly out to Colombia, South America, to bring back a few kilos of cocaine. The caller said his friend, who had just left to run a couple of errands, was the pilot and he was the co-pilot.

The caller went on to say that his pilot buddy was the one with the money, and the last few times they made the trip his pilot friend had brought back a few kilos of cocaine for a friend of his. The pilot began by asking the co-pilot to accompany him on the flight and, when they returned home, the pilot would give him between $500 and $1,000 just for going on the flight with him. The caller further stated that if I was going to pursue the case, I would have to hurry and act fast because he was facing time constraints.

I asked him for a little more information. "Did they have any junk or any drugs in the room?"

"Why?" he asked. "Are you looking to arrest us? Because if you are, all bets are off. You can forget I ever made this call."

"No," I said, "I just want to make certain that you're on the level and that no drugs are leaving the country. First of all, I don't know who you are. I would like to think you're honest, but maybe you're some yo-yo, or some kind of a nut, giving me a line of shit. Can you give me a sample of the stuff or something concrete so that I can open up a case file? It would help to solidify the investigation and give it greater legitimacy."

"Yes," he said, "I'll give you a sample of what we're bringing back. Look, I'm giving you a good case, but you're going to have to act quickly and get here as fast as you can. Like I told you, we're bringing back a couple of kilos of cocaine in a couple of days. But you're asking too many questions and we're wasting too much time. I'll give you about a half ounce of the stuff we're bringing back as a sample. Okay?"

I said, "Fine, but we'll have to talk about strategy for the delivery. Okay?"

"Fine," he said, "but you've got to hurry and get over here, alright. I don't want my friend coming back and hear that I'm having a conversation with you. I don't want him getting suspicious, so please, get over here as quick as you can."

"Just one more question and I'm on my way, okay? Why are you doing this? Are you just being a good citizen and doing your civic duty? Is this some sort of revenge? Is there money involved?"

"Look, I've done this several times now and we've been lucky so far, but frankly with each trip, I get more nervous and scared. Even though I'm making money with each trip, it's getting to the point where I'm really paranoid. I don't want to wait till our luck runs out. I just don't want to do it anymore. Okay?"

After jotting down the address he gave me, I hung up the phone and looked around to see if there was an available agent to go with me on the case, but no one had returned yet, not even the secretary. The office was still empty.

The pilot had stressed serious time constraints, so if I waited around for an agent to return, I might not get there on time. With the strong possibility that I was about to make a real big case, probably one of the biggest in New Orleans, there were really no options. The decision was an easy one. Just go and meet the caller co-pilot.

I was curious and somewhat baffled by the fact that all the time I was on the phone, there was no one in the office, not even the secretary, who's always there. Was it coincidental, or was it by design? What the hell was going on? Regardless, my focus was to deal with the situation at hand, and how I was going to handle the "Mississippi Pilots Investigation."

I was well aware that, since the Tijuana case, I had begun to withdraw, and my enthusiasm had waned. But no matter how I felt, whenever I knew I was in the process of initiating an interesting and potentially major case, my antennas would go up and the adrenaline would get going. It was like a jet ready for takeoff. Maybe, just maybe, this investigation was the catalyst that was going to be the renewal I needed. Perhaps my luck was about to change. I certainly hoped so.

When I arrived at the hotel by the airport, I knocked on the door and a tall white male, dressed in a pilot's uniform, opened the door. After an exchange of greetings, I reminded the man that I was the agent he'd spoken to on the phone. I proceeded to ask him for the sample he was going to give me, and he gave me a tin foil package containing a white, crystal-like powder. I secured the package and then informed him that I was going to search the room and their belongings, as we had agreed.

I opened the closet, and there were two jackets that appeared to be part of a pilot's uniform. I searched the closet and the jackets with negative results. I asked him to open his luggage as well as the pilot's. I searched his luggage and came up empty. However, while searching his partner's luggage, I found a small cellophane bag containing a white, crystal-like powder, similar to the white powder contained in the sample he'd given me.

As I was about to take the small bag, the co-pilot shouted, "No, you can't take that!"

"Why not?" I asked.

"Because that's for his own personal use, and if he discovers that the bag is missing, he's going to get highly suspicious and plans may go belly up. So, please, put it back. If you don't, then all bets are off. Now, please, put it back."

I put the bag back in the pilot's luggage, and the co-pilot urged me to leave. He said, "Look, you got your half ounce sample, you searched the place and luggage and found nothing. I told you that you're going to have a good case, but if you don't leave right now and my friend comes in, you're going to mess this up and blow the case open. So, please, leave."

We exchanged phone numbers, and I told him to call me just before they left Colombia so that I could plan accordingly for their return and the possible arrests at the airport. Upon leaving the room, I established surveillance by positioning myself in an area where I had a good vantage point to their room.

Shortly thereafter, I observed a white male in a pilot's uniform walking towards the hotel room. He knocked on the door and entered. Approximately fifteen minutes later, both men left the room carrying their luggage and walked towards the hotel parking lot. When I saw them get into a vehicle, I hurried back to my car, and came back to follow them, but by that time they were gone. When you're alone, you're obviously at a disadvantage, but the fact that I was handling the case by myself couldn't be helped.

I returned to the office and noticed everyone was there, including the secretary. I met with Jim Bland, the supervisor, and informed him of what had transpired. He was ecstatic. I told him there was no one in the office when the call came in, and because of time constraints, I had to go and meet with the co-pilot alone. I repeated that there was no one in the office, but I couldn't wait.

Bland said he was meeting with one of the supervisors from the New Orleans P.D., but he couldn't understand why there was no one in the office. Certainly, the secretary should have been there. "Nevertheless, you made a case, and it looks like a very good one, provided this co-pilot sticks to the plan and calls you when he's ready to return. Now that you got that half ounce sample, let's open up a case file. In the interim, we'll just have to wait until you hear from the co-pilot."

The following morning, I reported to work, and shortly after I arrived at the office, Bland approached me and informed me that District Supervisor (DS) I. Pappas and another District Supervisor (didn't know from where) wanted to see me, and that I should bring my daily reports with me. I asked Bland who Pappas was, and he said that Pappas was the DS of the Atlanta office, which oversaw the New Orleans office, but he didn't know where the other DS was from. Nonetheless, they were in his office and they wanted to see me, and I should bring my daily reports with me. Daily reports were the equivalent of a timesheet and a log of an agent's daily activities that must be filled out by every agent. I retrieved my daily reports and went to Bland's office to meet with the two supervisors.

Upon entering the office and seeing the two men, my jaw dropped as well as my daily reports, which fell on the floor. The two district supervisors were the same two pilots I had seen the day before. Pappas, the pilot, introduced himself as the DS from Atlanta, and the other man introduced himself as John Windham, DS of the FBN office in Seattle, Washington.

I froze momentarily, as I was stunned and shocked at what I saw and what I was experiencing. The two district supervisors, less than twenty-four hours ago, in their undercover assignment, had posed as pilots flying to Colombia to bring back a couple of kilos of cocaine. Windham was the co-pilot who had placed the call to the office and the one who let me in the room. He was the individual who gave me the sample of cocaine. Pappas was the pilot who I saw enter the hotel room after I had left.

After introductions, Pappas stated, "Sit down, Agent Gonzalez, and tell us what happened yesterday; where did you go, and what took place?"

"Did I hear you correctly?" I asked. "You want me to tell you what happened yesterday, what I did and where I went? You've got to be kidding. Is this some sort of a joke?"

"This is by no means a joke," Agent Pappas said. "You heard me, answer the question."

I replied, "Why are you asking me? You know better than I what happened. You were there. You're the architects of this whole scheme. Why don't you tell me what happened and why you did it? Why was this necessary? You don't have to be a genius to recognize that I was set up, so why don't you tell me why I was set up?"

"Sit down!" Agent Pappas shouted. "We'll ask the questions. You just answer them."

Bristling, I said, "I'll answer them when you tell me what this is all about. All right? Don't I have a right to know, or did I suddenly lose my rights? What about due process?"

Pappas, who was very curt, stated, "We're conducting an investigation into allegations of agent corruption in New York and that's why we're here. Now do you understand?"

"Agent corruption in New York?" I asked. "No, I don't understand. What the hell's that got to do with me? I left New York over a year ago when I was transferred to Miami. Subsequently, I was transferred here to New Orleans, which I'm still trying to figure out, so I don't know what you're talking about. But, it wouldn't surprise me if you guys had something to do with those transfers."

"Listen Agent, you don't seem to understand. We're not here to address unfortunate incidents that have happened to you. Understand? Therefore, I suggest you start answering the questions and keep those sarcastic comments to yourself. Otherwise, you might find yourself in more trouble."

Pappas went on. "First of all, you started your career in New York and you were there a number of years before your transfer to Miami. While in New York, you were a very good agent, became very popular, and so you're very familiar with most, if not all, the agents in New York. Now that you know why we're here, why don't you try to live up to your reputation and be a little more cooperative? Now, go on and tell us about yesterday. And again, for the record, we'll ask the questions, you just answer them."

"Well, I'll tell you what happened because there's no mystery or secrecy as to what took place yesterday. You know as well as I do. You guys orchestrated the whole thing. But you indicated that you're investigating allegations of agent corruption. Before I go on, tell me, who's made the allegations? Some agent? Some dirt bag informant trying to save his ass? Some insidious bastard who's trying to make a name for himself and wants money, or some lowlife who's looking for vengeance against the agents who nailed him?"

Pappas said, "You know as well as we do, that we're not at liberty to discuss that. That's not open for discussion, so let's go on."

"I figured that," I replied. "Well, yesterday afternoon I was in the office when the phone rang. No one else was in the office, not even the secretary, so I answered the call, and it was you," pointing to Windham. I repeated the story he'd given me over the phone regarding their flight to Colombia, when they were to bring back a few kilos of cocaine. I said, "Because you [again pointing to Windham] were faced with serious time constraints, you asked me to rush over. And because there was no one else in the office, I left alone and went to the hotel room where you were staying and you let me in."

As I spoke I was becoming aware of my own vulnerability and that I was being placed in a deep dark place; both with these men and my own emotional state. I was in more jeopardy than I had imagined and things were about to get worse. What happened next is a matter I have relived and rehashed several times without relief.

Before I could continue, I was quickly interrupted by Pappas, who stated rather authoritatively, "Mistake NUMBER ONE. Never go on an investigation alone. Always make certain there's another agent with you."

"What!?" I said. "Didn't I just tell you there was no one in the office at the time? I'm very much aware that you never go on an investigation alone. However, there was no one in the office when the call came in. Listen, if I had decided to wait for an agent to return to the office, there was a good chance that I would blow the case. What would you have done then?"

Windham retorted, "I'm not saying I wouldn't have done the same thing. We're just telling you that it's not supposed to be the way you want. You're a very good agent with a fine reputation. You should know better."

"Well," I said, "whenever an opportunity to make a case presents itself, the ideal situation is not always at hand, so you try to do the best that you can despite conditions or circumstances. It seems to me, that if you have the potential to make a big case like that, particularly in Mississippi where kilo cases are rare, then I would think that going to investigate by yourself would be called for because there are no agents to be found. Those are mitigating circumstances that should be considered, are they not?"

Windham said, "The answer is no. There are no mitigating circumstances. In such a case you don't go. Agent safety comes first and as to the case, you forget about it. Kilo cases come and go."

"Fine," I said. "I'll accept that because I subscribe to the same philosophy of agent safety comes first. But how do you reconcile the fact that whoever planned and ordered my being set up also ordered the office to be empty when the telephone call came in from you guys."

"Listen," I continued, "if the government had not implemented that plan, there would have been agents available and none of this would have occurred. However, by implementing this scheme, a situation was created that was designed for failure. Thus, you're offering a scenario I'm not prepared to accept."

Windham replied, "Regardless, what you must remember is that the safety of the agent is first and foremost. Therefore, if no one is around, you do not go despite the potential of the investigation. As I told you, forget about the case. You obviously see things differently, but that's policy. And I'm telling you, that can be construed as 'bad judgment.' Now, go on with what happened yesterday."

I continued and told them that upon entering the apartment, Windham gave me a sample of cocaine as we'd agreed to on the phone. Then I proceeded to search the room and luggage. I found a small bag of cocaine in Pappas's luggage, which I tried to take with me. But Windham said it was for his [Pappas] own personal use and insisted that I leave the bag in his luggage for fear that if he discovered it was missing, plans would go awry.

At this juncture, Pappas again interrupted by saying, "Mistake NUMBER TWO. Never let drugs go out of the country."

"What!?" I shouted. "Listen, any agent worth his salt would have done the same thing I did. If I take the bag with me, there's a good chance that I'll blow the case. On the other hand, letting a small bag go in exchange for a few kilos of cocaine is a deal I'll take every time. Look, if you go along with those rules, you'll never make a case, at least a decent one. Sure, there's always some Mickey Mouse investigation waiting to be initiated, but I prefer to stay away from those and focus my attention on worthwhile, meaningful investigations."

Pappas, who seemed to be annoyed and angered by my comments, replied, "Agent, I warned you, but you continue to dismiss or ignore what I say. As far as I'm concerned, you have a very cavalier attitude and you're cocky and stubborn. Your disregard in following orders and ignoring rules and regulations and your sarcastic vitriol during this investigation does not bode well for you. Now, let's review your daily reports."

Unable to find any form of corrupt activity during their undercover assignment, they were now looking for something to hang their hat on. In most cases, when trying to pin something on an agent, as a last resort, the only place to look was the daily reports. Everyone knew that you can nail the Pope on a daily report.

As I turned the pages and sifted through the contents, the first question I was asked regarded the mileage on my car. The mileage I had listed on the report said it was 43,000 miles. "How is it," Pappas asked, "that the odometer reads 48,000 miles?"

I said that I may have inadvertently listed the wrong digit, an eight instead of a three, on the daily report. In view of the discrepancy, was I guilty of lying or providing erroneous or deceitful information? If so, to what end? For what purpose?

Pappas quickly stated, "Agent, I'm telling you again, we'll ask the questions and you answer them. Do you understand?"

"Yes, sir, I understand, but how do you treat that discrepancy?"

"Well," Pappas explained, "it could be an extension of your carefree attitude, or perhaps you're lying, and if so, why? Are you trying to cover up using a government vehicle for personal matters, or is there some other reason? When questioned about it, you obviously didn't remember and became very defensive."

"I get defensive because I find this to be very petty. Picayune. Let me say that I honestly don't see the correlation between the mileage listed on the report and the corruption you are investigating."

Pappas replied, "We'll make that determination. Now, look closely on this particular day of the week where you indicate being in the office between the hours of 11:00 a.m. through 2:00 p.m. What were you doing in the office?"

I replied, "I was doing administrative work, paperwork in general, reviewing fugitive files, going over pending cases, answering phones and such. A portion of time was also allotted for lunch."

Pappas then asked, "If you were supposed to be in the office doing administrative work and having lunch, what was your car doing by the Quarter on Poydras and Bourbon by the LSU campus?"

I told them that on that particular day, I had gone to the registrar's office at the campus of Louisiana State University (LSU) because I wanted to register for a course.

"Well," Pappas said, "you do realize that you're not supposed to use government vehicles for personal business, only for official business."

"Isn't that the height of pettiness?" I asked.

"If in fact you did go to LSU to register for a course, why not reflect the information in your daily report? Once again, why lie? What are you trying to hide or cover up? You see what I mean, Agent? You don't seem concerned about any of this, and your attitude is one of indifference."

"First of all," I said, "I'm not lying, and the reason I'm not concerned is because I haven't done anything wrong, much less illegal. I'm not that type of person. But you seem to be enjoying this exercise in futility."

"There you go again, with your cocky and sarcastic attitude," Pappas stated.

"Maybe it's your refusal to accept the truth," I shot back.

"Listen, I think we've heard enough of your philosophical remarks. Now, let's get on with New York," Pappas said.

"What about New York?" I asked.

He quickly rattled off the names of several agents I had worked with up there.

I said, "Yes."

"What can you tell me about them?"

"Listen, all I can tell you is that I consider myself very fortunate to have worked with the best agents in the country, and I learned a great deal from them. It's been an honor and a pleasure to have worked with those guys."

"Did any of them ever approach you about making money on the side?"

"What do you mean by that?" I asked.

Pappas explained. "Like giving drugs to informants and letting them sell the stuff for you."

"Never!" I snapped. "The agents I worked with were not like that. They were sharp street agents who were honest, dedicated, and extremely conscientious."

"What about extortion? Did any of them ever ask you to join them while they took money from individuals forcibly?"

Upon hearing this, I shouted angrily, "What!? You've got to be kidding."

I was enraged and told him I found this repulsive. "Listen, if you're really interested in looking into extortion, why don't you reach out to the Miami office and inquire about an informant or a guy by the name of J.C. Martin, or Marty. When I was there, Marty, supposedly an informant with ties to organized crime in the Miami Beach area was assigned to take me on the Strip where he was going to introduce me to some big shots with the hope of my making a good case. As we get near the Strip, Marty asks me to join him in shaking down someone in a dark street. I refused to take part in illegal acts. That's not what I'm all about and that's not what this job is all about. I laced into the guy and refused to work with him. Are you ever informed of those incidents? And, if so, do you investigate them with the same fervor as when you're investigating an agent?"

"And in addition, subsequent to that incident while working undercover, I met and became friendly with a Mexican drug dealer [Marcos Valdez] from Tijuana whose uncle [Jorge Favela] was the source of supply. I gained Valdez's confidence, and he invited me to go to Tijuana with him. We go to Tijuana, but I couldn't purchase any drugs because the Agency wouldn't approve the OAF any more than they approved surveillance. So, I went on my own."

"Then, upon my return from Tijuana, they took the case away from me, and I was directed to surrender the case to the LA office for reasons of logistics. I didn't buy the bullshit then, and I don't buy it now. Why don't you investigate those incidents? Frankly, I'm convinced that it was for the same reason I was transferred to Miami and then to New Orleans. They were more interested in setting me up. It didn't work in Miami with that shakedown incident, so they figure a transfer to New Orleans might be more appropriate. I don't know why they're doing this, but I can tell you this. If it's based on allegations of corruption, the allegations are baseless and without foundation. It's all a vicious smear. You don't take the word of the agents, but you place your trust in what these lowlife sleazebags have to say."

I truly was on fire and could not contain myself, "I think it's a moral outrage and absolutely sinful that you guys are sent on these undercover missions to deliberately destroy the character and reputation of agents whose integrity is a non-issue and whose professionalism and capability is unquestioned."

Angered by my comments, Pappas stated that I was lacking in discipline and sound judgment. Furthermore, he said I was not the most cooperative of individuals as I became very hostile and defensive in answering certain challenging questions.

I became even more upset and launched into a tirade. I said to him, "Listen, I don't doubt that allegations were made by some drug dealing scumbag or some fucking lowlife sleaze ball for reasons best known to themselves, albeit, I can guess why. Meanwhile, a group of inspectors like you and your supervisor lose all objectivity, forget all about due process, and lend credence to those bastards by investigating agents that they mention."

"I'd like to know why there wasn't a background investigation conducted on those that made the allegations? No, you guys are sent here on a mission by some overzealous individual who loves this shit and is looking to make a name for himself."

I was on a roll. "And in my particular case, they didn't just get one ordinary undercover agent to investigate, but they went the elitist route by getting two district supervisors for their mission. They got one from Atlanta and the other one from as far as Seattle, Washington, to come down to New Orleans in pursuit of their investigation of 'Agent Corruption in New York.' I guess they thought I was a key figure from the Genovese or Gambino crime families, which normally require in-depth investigation by stellar investigators."

I was glaring straight into their eyes now and nothing for the moment could have held me back. "Well, let's see, you guys, two district supervisors, tried to set me up, and what do you come up with? Nothing. Your scheme backfires. Why? Because there is nothing. There's no corruption. It doesn't exist. The only thing you found was two minor violations. Finally, since you couldn't find anything, as a last resort, you go through the daily reports. And you come across two administrative infractions. Therefore, after conducting the investigation, all you came up with were four Mickey Mouse infractions—two during the course of the investigation or setup, and two upon review of the daily reports. These were harmless infractions or violations that were discussed and gone over during the interview, none of which had anything to do with corruption. Job well done, gentlemen."

"That's it," Pappas said, as he looked over to Windham. "He's suspended without pay. Do you agree?" Windham nodded accordingly. The indignant duo did not hesitate to tell me I was being suspended. Needless to say, I was shocked. I was livid. I became enraged and launched into a new angry sermon.

"Notwithstanding your unprofessional methods, you conduct an investigation into alleged corruption and all you come up with is four harmless infractions, truly an exercise in futility. And for that I'm suspended without pay. That's obscene. This isn't about corruption, it's about power, a false sense of power. In essence, this is a crock of shit. I realize you guys think you are just doing your job. And I don't know if it's one person or a group or committee, but whoever sent you here is an overzealous bastard who's morbidly insane of his own importance. They are so enveloped in this aura of grandeur that they've lost sight of all objectivity. What about a hearing? What about due process? What about the human element? This is not only repulsive, it's a fucking disgrace."

I tried to calm myself, but my anguish was so beyond that at that moment. Finally I asked, "Is this investigation over?"

Pappas said, "The New Orleans phase is over, but we're not completely done. We have to talk to more people. However, I must tell you that your comments during your 'soliloquy' did not help you very much."

"Well," I said, "you'll be interested to know that I'm not only finished with expressing my feelings that you label a 'soliloquy,' but I'm finished with this agency. I've always been a team player, but it appears this team is fragmented and it's every man for himself. Well, it becomes apparent that I'm no longer a part of the team. In that case, you'll have my credentials in the morning."

I left the office, and although I was mentally exhausted and physically drained, I went to church to sit, meditate, do a bit of introspection, and find some inner peace.

While at church, I shed a few tears and began asking myself some questions. What the hell did I just do? Why did I react that way? That was more than an overreaction. My behavior was completely antithetical to my persona. That was not me. It was a whole different person. What happened? Is my ego so sensitive, so fragile, that I went beyond indignation? They had nothing on me. Sure, there were allegations, but that means nothing. The allegations must have been equally as nebulous as the investigation itself, which revealed nothing.

I went home and informed my wife of what had transpired. Consistent with her love and support, she cried and was quite understanding and very supportive. But after shedding a few tears, she launched into her own tirade, as she asked, "Why? Why did you make this so easy for them? You loved that job. You were passionate about what you did. They're investigating corruption and you're not a corrupt person, so there's nothing to be concerned about. You're normally a cool guy under pressure, so why did you let it affect you this way? What prompted you to resign? I think that's unfair, not just to me and the girls, but to yourself. What will you do now? What will we do?"

"I don't know," I said. "Everything happened so fast. But their innuendo, their off-handed remarks got to me. It was a reaction, then an overreaction. But, not to worry, I'll figure something out."

The following morning, I met with them and surrendered my credentials. I was in a somber mood, so there was very little talking. I filled out all the necessary forms, and as I was about to leave the office when Jim Bland, the agent in charge, asked if he could have a word with me.

We moved to a private area where he told me he was sorry to see me leave. He went on to say that he'd spoken to other agents he knew in other cities and they spoke very highly of me.

He said I was a good agent and more than likely, we probably would have made a good team. He further stated that he had a good attorney and he felt strongly that I should challenge them. He also felt certain I could win the case and get reinstated. He told me to stay in touch.

We shook hands, and I left the building. While I considered going back to the investigators and having perhaps a rational discourse with them on the entire matter, something inside me would not allow it. Maybe it was the macho thing which I'm sure, as a Latino, I have traces of, or perhaps it was foolish pride. Nevertheless, it was not the way to end a career, albeit short-lived, that I loved.

Later on, I called Ben Fitzgerald in New York to advise him of what had happened, but he was on vacation. I called my good friend Joe Casale, whose immediate response was "Don't worry about a thing. You'll get through this, and I'll help you get back on your feet. Let me know when you'll be coming to New York, and I'll pick you up at the airport."

Subsequently, I returned to New York with my wife and children, realizing that my confrontation with FBN officials ended with my decision to resign abruptly. The sad fact was that I had not been fired, but merely suspended without pay.

While the inspectors may have reacted abruptly, because they were unable to find any evidence of wrong doing, it was I who over-reacted. I had neglected to check my ego at the door and I came to realize that misplaced bravado is all nonsense, if not stupid. I had put myself first without thinking about my wife and children who have always come first.

Nonetheless, I felt terrible. I had let my family down. I had taken a bad fall. And the best thing, in fact the only thing to do, was pick myself up and move forward. The time had come to start the process over and embark on a new career.

29

Association of Former Federal Narcotic

Agents

(AFFNA – 1984)

In 1984, a group of retired Federal Narcotic Agents got together in Washington, D.C. and founded an organization for retired and former agents of DEA and its predecessor agencies. The purpose of the organization has remained the same since inception - to provide and preserve goodwill and friendship amongst former federal narcotic agents, assist its members with executive job placement, secure health and life insurance programs and aid and support DEA.

Subsequently, the establishment of other Chapters throughout the country followed, including the New York Chapter which was founded in 1985. Still bitter and upset over my experience with FBN in New Orleans, I had no desire in becoming an AFFNA member nor did I have any interest in attending any of its meetings. However, one day I ran into an old friend and former agent Dick Holborow, who urged and encouraged me to attend one of the Chapter meetings in New York, but I declined. Aware that I still had mixed feelings towards the agency, Holborow continued in his efforts to convince me to attend a meeting if for no other reason than to exchange greetings, break bread and share some war stories with some of the guys I was truly friendly with but had not seen in a very long time.

After some persistent, but friendly persuasion, I finally attended a meeting that, I must admit, made me feel at ease and a bit more comfortable. I recognized some of the Agents in attendance, but upper most in my mind was the hope of seeing a tough, street smart, Latino agent named Louie Diaz, whom I had recommended for the job a few years before.

After my fallout with FBN, I left New Orleans and returned home to New York where I got a job as Director of a Center for Adolescent Youth in Williamsburg, Brooklyn.

Louie Diaz and I had met while working together at the Center and we quickly became friends. As two Latinos from Brooklyn, we had a lot in common. He was from the Red Hook Section, and I was from Sunset Park - both predominantly Italian and Irish communities albeit culturally and ethnically mixed.

It was the time of "West Side Story" and frankly these were tough neighborhoods where you had to assert yourself. If you wanted to play sports, make friends, go to parties and have fun, you adapted. And that meant, fighting with guys in your neighborhood who frequently provoked the fight but eventually became your friends. Now that you were friends, you and your new buddies found yourselves fighting with other groups of guys from different neighborhoods.

Admittedly, most of the fighting was territorial or scuffles over one of the gals in your neighborhood who was going out with one of the guys from a rival group. Nevertheless, one thing was clear, there was little room for those who didn't subscribe to that philosophy, or whose behavior was non aggressive and where passive acceptance was the norm. Clearly, one learned to adapt, and the process of adaptation led to acculturation.

Growing up in that environment enabled us to become immersed in both Latino and Anglo cultures. We often kidded each other as to how we came to fit in with the guys in the neighborhood and our respective communities.

As a Spaniard, I often teased Louie by referring to him as, 'Gallego.' Invariably, he'd get very up tight and with obvious indignation, would quickly reply, "Hey, I'm Asturiano, not Gallego, understand."

The remarks are not demeaning nor do they take a disparaging view of any one person or group. In fact, it's like a source of ethnic pride as well as geographic or territorial pride - similar to the attitude and behavior manifested by sports rivals, (e.g.) N.Y. Yankees vs. Boston Red Sox; South vs. North, etc. It's quite prevalent and socially acceptable in our society and most often seen in the world of sports where there are traditionally strong rivalries.

Louie Diaz wanted very much to be an agent and I wanted to help him. However, due to the falling out I had with the Agency, I hesitated to recommend him for fear it might work against him. But his constant reminders and his fervent desire to be an agent was so definitive it left me little choice, so I recommended him to Jim Hunt, another old friend still on the job and a highly respected Group Leader.

The hiring process was not an easy one for Louie as he ran into a few road blocks. But, he persevered and was eventually sworn in. He went on to make a name for himself by making a good number of cases including some high profile investigations.

I spoke to him on several occasions and he told me things were going well and he was very happy. He also pointed out that he'd taken quite a bit of abuse from agents who knew me well, but often reminded him that he was Louie D. and not Louie G. He went on to say that it was like an albatross around his neck. I quickly informed him that he had to learn to dismiss the exaggerations made by those agents as the comments were made in the name of fun. They were just kidding him and having some fun.

As part of his early success as an Agent, Louie had also been involved in extra-curricular activities by representing DEA in the "Mini-Olympics," an Inter-Agency Sponsored Sports Program. He competed in the Program's Boxing Tournament and won the Middle- Weight Championship. I congratulated him and told him I was very proud of him. He thanked me over and over again for being his mentor and for the counseling provided.

But more importantly, he thanked me for being his friend and for that, he was extremely grateful and would never forget. While I deeply appreciated his comments, I made it clear that it was he who had done the preparation, it was he who had adapted to the process and most of all, it was he who had heretofore achieved such lofty goals. He was quite happy and further added that his biggest wish had come true - he had been transferred to the Los Angeles Office in California where he subsequently retired.

The relationship has been tantamount to that of older brother/ little brother and despite the fact that I live in New York and he resides in California, we've remained friends and continue to stay in touch. Unquestionably, the bond and the friendship has been and remains steadfast since inception.

I continued to attend AFFNA meetings in New York and even took part in several discussions, raising some issues I felt were relevant and applicable to the group. As a result, when election time came around, my name was placed in nomination for Secretary of the Chapter and, surprisingly, I was elected. More surprisingly however, was the fact that after serving a couple of terms as Secretary I was elected Chairman of the Chapter.

Now that I was Chairman, I realized I had to forget what had occurred in the past and focus my attention on my role as Chairman as well as the path the Chapter was going to take.

Despite feelings of ambivalence towards FBN, I was not about to shirk my responsibilities. It was no secret that animosity between DEA and FBN still existed. Therefore, it seemed

Imperative to me that one of the goals of the N.Y. Chapter could certainly be, to dispel the notion that there was any form of animosity between members or try to invalidate that perception.

To see a good number of FBN agents join the Chapter, was, I believe, a good beginning toward that goal. Whether you were former FBN or DEA, we were now comrades. And a new form of camaraderie would hopefully bring about better understanding, more unity and much better relations amongst us all.

I reached out to a bunch of FBN guys, all of whom were contemporaries and good friends, to help me in that effort. They did not just retire from FBN, but went on to become highly successful individuals in their own respective careers.

Joe Casale, of Sinatra fame, went to work in the insurance industry where he prospered and became a prominent business executive.

Tony Falanga, an attorney by profession, left FBN to practice law. Subsequently, he was elected for District Judge in Hempstead, Long Island, and after a few terms as District Judge, he ran for higher office and was again victorious. He was now, a New York State Supreme Court Judge in Nassau County, Long Island.

Frank Iopolo, despite several personal problems, became a successful real estate attorney, and Jerry Weinberg, President of a Travel/Tourism company and co-owner of a hotel in San Martin, also joined the Chapter.

At the time, Chuck Leya, once "Range Officer" for the New York Field Division, in charge of training and qualifying all agents at the Pistol Range, was now an accountant for a private firm and, upon joining the Chapter, became the Treasurer. Florence Trani, Secretary to George Belk, the District Supervisor of the New York Office, also joined the bandwagon and became the chapter's Administrative Assistant. Norman Matuozzi and Ben Fitzgerald from The Court House Squad of the New York Office were among the first to join.

Collectively the aforementioned group, contemporaries all, along with DEA agent Nick Aleva, who had recently retired, contributed largely towards increasing membership from the original sixteen (16) to approximately seventy members. By creating and participating in a variety of social events, recreational events and aiding and supporting DEA, the Chapter got a lot of exposure and visibility.

Our most notable achievement however, was the creation of the "Agent of the Year" award, given annually to agents from the New York/New Jersey Field Divisions who were recognized for their outstanding performance throughout the year.

At an awards luncheon held every spring at a local restaurant, the selected winners received their awards. In addition, they also received a trip to San Martin for each recipient and his/her spouse or companion. The trip was sponsored by Jerry Weinberg, and included a stay in his hotel.

As a very popular and successful program, "The Agent of the Year Award" became a model for other chapters to develop or replicate. In fact, it has become part of the National Chapter's annual national convention. Approximately twenty years later, the N. Y. Chapter joined forces with a newly established Chapter in the New Jersey area and it was called The New York/New Jersey Chapter of AFFNA.

By this time, there seemed to be sense of a camaraderie between FBN and DEA agents and it manifested itself in their attitude and behavior towards one another. But, there were still traces of animosity and a disparaging view taken by some towards FBN for reasons best known to themselves, and so, the stigma remained. But that would soon be a thing of the past.

30

The New AFNA

In 2016, the AFFNA Board decided to amend the organization's title by dropping one of the (F) letters, thereby removing
the word "former" from its abbreviated title. Previously,
membership was restricted to retired DEA Agents and administrative personnel. The new AFNA membership was now open to
active agents yet retired and "Task Force" members who had been
part of the DEA enforcement effort for a very long time but were
heretofore ineligible for membership.

At the annual conference in October 12-15, 2016 at Hilton
Head, Carolina, the newly revised AFNA went a long way
towards rectifying that situation and removing whatever stigma
and ill-feelings might still exist. At its organizational meeting, the
AFNA Board of Trustees paid tribute to its predecessor agency
FBN, all former FBN agents and acknowledged their dedication,
commitment and their noteworthy contribution to drug enforcement. At special ceremonies, FBN Agents were given an award—
a replica of the original FBN shield and a gift box containing (6)
shields in the form of a lapel pin, representing all of DEA's predecessor agencies since inception.

Consensus among DEA members was that it was a great gesture
on the organization's part, albeit long overdue. The feeling among
FBN Agents was that it was "Better late than Never" situation. As
to the government's view on the entire matter, it was tantamount to
Shakespeare's comments of "All's well that Ends Well."

References

Newspaper Articles

The N. Y. Times, August 1, 1961 - Gennaro Salzano
    Investigation—"Two Held in Slaying Here"
Newsday - August 1961 – "Dope Pusher Slain, Body Dumped"

Court Documents

United States Court of Appeals -vs- Gennaro Salzano,
    defendant - Appellant, 241 F. 2nd 849 - (2nd Circuit 1957),
    Docket No. 24061– Appeal denied.
Court of Appeals for the 2nd Circuit 348 F 2nd 316 United
    States of America; Appellee -vs- Pardo-Bolland and Rene
    Bruchon – Appeal denied.

About the Author

A ngel L. Gonzalez is an adopted child of a devoted, loving and caring mother and a father who—as a strict, disciplined career military man—was the complete antithesis of his mom. His parents left Puerto Rico near the end of World War Two and settled in Brooklyn, N.Y. seeking a better way of life. Angel, who more often than not is called Louie G; and Ango to others, was raised in the Sunset Park section of Brooklyn, N.Y. However, he's quick to remind you that despite growing up in Brooklyn, he's always been and remains a rabid Yankee fan, which doesn't sit too well with the Brooklyn folk.

A product of the NYC public school system, he grew up playing competitive sports and was equally as adept in dancing, particularly Latin dance music. As to his indulgence in sports, he's quick to remind you of how proud he is of having the distinction of having played baseball against Hall of Famer Sandy Koufax and Fred Wilpon, President of the N.Y. Mets.

In fact, he'll remind you that not too many people are aware that Sandy Koufax played 1st. Base and Fred Wilpon was a Pitcher for the Lafayette H.S. Baseball Team in Brooklyn. He'll further remind you that not even the World Wide Web is aware that Koufax got a Basketball Scholarship to the University of Cincinnati, and Wilpon got a Baseball Scholarship to the University of Michigan. He also played against Wilpon, who was a star pitcher with the "Blue Jays" a sandlot team in the Kiwanus League in Brooklyn. The rest is history.

A graduate of Fordham University at Lincoln Center in Manhattan, he's a veteran of the U.S. Amy and served in post-war Korea. After military service, he spent most of his adult life working in (3) separate careers. First, with The Federal Bureau of Narcotics (FBN), which is where this story begins. Notwithstanding the fact that it was a short-lived career, he's also very proud and honored to have been one of the very first few "Latinos" with FBN at a time when it wasn't fashionable to have ethnics on board.

It begins with his service in the New York Office where his dedication and integrity made him one of the most reliable and successful undercover agents of his era.

As one of the very few Latino Agents in FBN at the time, the story follows his adventures as an undercover agent, totally immersed in activities that filled the headlines of major newspapers—from the French Connection Case to the arrest and imprisonment of several diplomats, namely Pardo Bolland, Mexican Ambassador to Bolivia; Jose Arizti, a member of the Uruguayan Foreign Ministry and Rene Bruchon, former Ambassador to Switzerland. His role as a key figure in the initial battles with major drug traffickers is a matter of record. But, his tenure within the agency was not always behind the scenes successes. A sudden transfer to the Miami Office, followed by a couple of mysterious, peculiar incidents leave him completely baffled and perplexed. Moreover, while working undercover in Tijuana, Mexico building a case against one of Tijuana's drug kingpins, he learns of his inexplicable transfer—this time—to the New Orleans, La. Office. He soon finds himself embroiled in internal controversies and unfounded allegations of agent corruption that were subsequently investigated and proven to be groundless. Nonetheless, it brings him into direct conflict with his superiors leading him to question his motivation and commitment to the agency, resulting in a short-lived career.

Subsequently, he returns to New York with his family and embarks on a new career in Private Industry as Manager of a

Venture Capital Company and subsidiary of International Paper Co., a (Fortune 500) Company and one of the largest Pulp and Paper Manufacturing firms in the country. Years later, the company decides to relocate its Corporate Headquarters in Memphis, Tn. While he's asked to go, he declines and returns to the Federal Government, conducting background investigations for the Department of Defense.

Several years later he's asked to join the New York State Gaming Commission, the agency that regulates all forms of gambling in the State of New York including Thoroughbred Racing. After a distinguished career as the Investigator for the Commission at the three racetracks in New York (Aqueduct; Belmont and Saratoga) he brings closure to his third career with the thought that there are yet more worlds to explore.

Awards/Citations

Special Service Awards from the U.S. Treasury Department - Bureau of Narcotics - for noteworthy contribution in the following investigations:

- The French Connection Case (1962). U.S. Treasury Department - Bureau of Narcotics

- Ambassador Investigation (Pardo Bolland, Mexican Ambassador to Bolivia, and Jose Arizti.

- Member of the Uruguayan Foreign Ministry). U.S. Treasury Department - Bureau of Narcotics.